MW01003066

Imitating Jesus

Love, Friendship, and Disciple-Making

Lewie Clark

with

Tim Grissom

WestBow
PRESS
A DIVISION OF THOMAS NELSON

Unless otherwise indicated, all Scripture quotations are from the HOLY BIBLE, NEW INTERNATIONAL VERSION®. NIV®. Copyright© 1973, 1978, 1984 by International Bible Society. Used by permission of Zondervan. All rights reserved.

Names and details in some anecdotes and stories have been changed to protect the identities of the persons involved.

Requests for permission to make copies of this publication should be sent to: IconChicago@yahoo.com.

WestBow Press books may be ordered through booksellers or by contacting:

WestBow Press
A Division of Thomas Nelson
1663 Liberty Drive
Bloomington, IN 47403
www.westbowpress.com
1-866-928-1240

Because of the dynamic nature of the Internet, any web addresses or links contained in this book may have changed since publication and may no longer be valid. The views expressed in this work are solely those of the author and do not necessarily reflect the views of the publisher, and the publisher hereby disclaims any responsibility for them.

ISBN: 978-1-4497-4386-4 (sc)
ISBN: 978-1-4497-4387-1 (e)

Library of Congress Control Number: 2012904985

Printed in the United States of America

WestBow Press rev. date: 04/18/2012

Contents

Acknowledgments ix

Introduction xi

1. Strikeouts and Second Chances 1

2. In the Company of Disciples 5

   Justin's Story, Part 1 13

3. What Is God Like? 15

   Justin's Story, Part 2 23

4. That's Where I Belong 25

   Chris's Story 33

5. Hospitality 35

   Jamie's Story 43

6. The Discipleship Relationship 51

   Nate's Story 59

7. The Timeline 61

   Jeremy's Story, Part 1 69

8. Defining Moments 71

   Jeremy's Story, Part 2 79

9. Heart-Mining: 200 Questions to Ask Your Disciple 81

   Brent's Story 91

10. Finding Your Disciple 93

    Danny's Story 101

Epilogue 105

Notes 107

To my father and mother, Lewis and Marjorie Clark, who have faithfully followed Jesus over sixty years.

The earthly ministry of Jesus of Nazareth constitutes the one time in the history of humanity when heaven fully and finally came to earth. In Matthew, Mark, Luke, and John, we have the opportunity to see the question *What is God like?* answered in the flesh-and-blood world in which we live. During His incarnation Jesus not only procured our way to heaven. He also shows us how to live on earth. Now we can pattern our lives after Jesus.
—Joseph H. Hellerman

Acknowledgments

None of this would be possible without the faith and love of my dad and mom.

Taylor and Jimmye Gardner not only introduced me to the heart of disciple-making but gave me the privilege of the experience of such love. I have often wondered where my life would be without their influence.

When I was diagnosed with cancer, Steve Craig led the charge along with the other board members of Icon Ministries (Justin Bertram, Stuart Cearley, Chris Coleman, Randy Ferguson, Merlin Hagan, and Paul Mattson) to make this book possible. I am grateful.

I would be remiss not to thank my spiritual family in Chicago. Together we have labored for the past eight years seeking the kingdom of God.

Tim Grissom says the most important thing about a writer is that he has something to say. I had something to say and Tim helped me to say it more effectively, for which I am grateful.

I wish I could thank by name all the disciples who, through the years, have brought great joy to my life. This is their story.

Introduction

This is a book about loving well, building friendships, and making followers of Jesus. It came about through the influence of several longtime friends who for years urged me to write down how I "do ministry" and two new friends who escalated the priority of doing so: age and cancer.

While young I did not give much thought to how I did ministry because there were many exciting opportunities before me, coupled with plenty of time. I knew that if one approach did not work then I could always try something else. I have since worked at a Christian college, traveled with an itinerant ministry, participated in church start-ups, and served in both traditional and contemporary churches—all the while being involved in myriad ministry strategies and initiatives.

Age has given me the opportunity to look back over thirty years of ministry to determine what lasted and what did not. This is the story of how I have simplified my life to do the main thing, make disciples of Jesus.

The day I was diagnosed with cancer, I walked out of my doctor's office in a daze, went across the street, and sat down on a park bench. In those moments I realized that what mattered was God's love for me, my love for him, the people who loved me, and those whom I loved. I had a new understanding of what John meant when he wrote: "God is love. Whoever lives in love lives in God, and God in him" (1 John 4:16).

I have a new singular devotion . . . to love well. *That's* how disciples are made.

1

Strikeouts and Second Chances

The drive from my apartment in Little Rock to the campus in Arkadelphia took an hour and fifteen minutes—long enough to give myself a scolding, adding it to the one from the night before.

How could I have missed it?

I was on my way back to Ouachita Baptist University in hopes of finding Kyle and getting a second chance to listen to his story. Since he had asked me to disciple him, we had been meeting a few times each month, usually on campus. In fact, we had just met the night before when he had shared a story with me from his childhood. And I had missed the significance of it.

The story was this:

> Kyle was eight years old and a player for the Tigers, a Little League baseball team. They were a good team, known for winning games and league championships.
>
> That's what made Kyle so nervous. In his mind he was an average player on his best days and the weakest member of the team. Eight-year-old boys don't admit to feelings like that, though. They just hope the day never comes when they're the goat that costs the team a win. And they dream about the day when they score the winning run.

Well, that day came for Kyle, the perfect setup for heroism—final inning, team down by one run, two outs, bases loaded. Kyle was at bat. A base hit could win the game.

Kyle struck out.

That game, that strikeout, was a defining moment in Kyle's life. He had tried to tell me so the night before, but I hadn't heard. I'd broken a cardinal rule of discipleship: Listen with your ears *and your heart.* So I was driving back, hoping Kyle would have time to visit with me and praying we could talk about that story again. This time, I promised God and myself, I would listen. *Really* listen.

Arriving on campus, I set out to find Kyle. I knew his usual hangouts, so it didn't take long. He was surprised to see me just the day after meeting with him, so we sat down at an outdoor table and I jumped in.

"Kyle," I said, "that Little League story you told me yesterday is really important to you, isn't it?"

"Yes, it is," he replied.

And I missed the point, didn't I?"

"Yes you did."

I appreciated his honesty, and he graciously told me the story again. This time he ended by saying: "I know it may sound crazy, but my life has revolved around that one incident; I can't seem to shake it. Every day I ask myself if I have what it takes to make it."

Inside this handsome, athletic college senior was an eight-year-old boy slumping back to the dugout, feeling like a failure and a disappointment. He'd been feeling that way most of the fourteen or so years since that Little League game.

Now I knew where to go in our discipleship relationship. Kyle was wounded. He needed his perspective realigned and his confidence bolstered. He needed someone to believe in him and to assure him that his life had purpose.

People who see themselves as failures are sure that others see them that way too. We're surrounded by people like Kyle—wounded people who live in the shadows of shame. They've fallen prey to their own strikeouts and wake up every day wondering if they have what it takes, if their life has any value, and what their purpose for living really is. Some of them wonder if they've become God's afterthought, or if he even cares they exist.

Given that, the disciple-maker's core mission is to help the disciple know—really know—that God loves him.

Where have all the disciple-makers gone?

I fear we're losing the simplicity of discipleship, resulting in disciple-makers becoming an endangered species. I can't count the number of people who have approached me over the years, wanting to help people they know meet Christ and grow in spiritual maturity, yet feeling that they're not up to the challenge. These are solid people, grounded in their faith, and successful in most areas of life. Many of them are, or have been, leaders in their community, business, and church. But when it comes to disciple-making—a job that Christ clearly gave to all of his followers—they're stumped.

This is what I tell every one of them: disciple-making comes down to love and friendship. Get those two basic things right, and you can make disciples.

In the chapters that follow, I'll share some practical suggestions (e.g., 200 questions to ask your disciple, how to help your disciple discover how God has been at work in his or her life, and ways to recognize teachable moments in your disciple's life), but above all I'll emphasize love and friendship.

That's what Jesus did.

A little clarification

I want to clarify three things before moving ahead. Information like this is often tucked away in the introduction and many times gets missed by the reader. But I want to explain them here to help you understand where I'm coming from and why I say certain things the way that I do.

1. *My disciples are not really my disciples.* You'll notice that I often refer to a person as *my* disciple. I recognize that they're not *my* disciples in the literal sense, but Christ's. I only use this term to draw the distinction that this person is someone with whom I've entered into a significant disciple-making relationship.

2. *Salvation should not be presumed.* When thinking about disciple-making, we often picture those who have already placed their faith in Christ and want help in their spiritual growth. However, this is not always the case. Through the years I've worked with several individuals who came to faith in Christ *during* our discipleship and not before it. I've also worked with many who, through the course of our discipleship, concluded that they were not truly a Christian even though they had thought they were when we began.

3. *Most of my stories are about men.* Because I am a single man and have never been married, most of my discipleship relationships have been with men. Not all, but most. Discipleship gets quite personal, and it can be difficult (and in my opinion sometimes inappropriate) for a man to disciple a woman or a woman to disciple a man. So if I refer mostly to *he* or *him*, or if my stories and examples seem disproportionately male, you'll know why.

With that, let's talk more about disciple-making, a lesson I learned, and a course correction I made after twenty-plus years.

2

In the Company of Disciples

Several years ago I began looking more closely at the discipling methods of Jesus. I was intrigued by the way that he used both one-on-one encounters and group settings to develop the spiritual maturity of his followers. Until that time I had concentrated almost entirely on one-on-one relationships, so I decided to make some changes.

I invited several of the guys I was discipling to dinner at my apartment. I was not an experienced dinner host, to say the least, but cuisine and entertainment were not my objectives. I wanted these guys to meet one another and hopefully become friends. I believed we would develop a group dynamic of love and of encouraging one another forward in our mutual faith. After all, this is a hallmark of true discipleship: "By this all men will know that you are my disciples, if you love one another" (John 13:35).

The evening was . . . disappointing. When the last guy left, I remember thinking, *Not only do these guys not love one another, some of them can't even get along.*

What was I doing wrong?

I realized that, sitting in a Starbucks, a guy could snow me by giving the impression that all his relationships were healthy. But in a community with other believers, his relational fault lines were exposed and his true character was revealed. So over the next several months, I began coaching the guys individually on how to love the others and how to receive love from them. This brought several of my guys to a new and unexpected level of heart-change as they began to uncover old fears and insecurities. Some of them did not believe they could ever be loved, and this explained why it was nearly impossible for them to give love. They were dragged down with raw memories, but God was drawing them out of the dark corners by presenting them with opportunities for authentic friendships.

This group approach was working.

Let me clarify, I didn't *replace* one-on-one discipleship with a group or community approach; I simply *added* one to the other. I found that combining the two brought greater health to all involved, and even affected some who were hanging around but not directly participating as they began to be influenced by the life-change going on within our group. I've since discovered that this is not uncommon, that there is often an "outer ring" of individuals who observe, listen, and learn, but are not as intimately involved as others are. We can see this in the ministry of Christ as he built an extended discipling community in Galilee beyond his twelve men.

Although the gospel writers do not give us a direct description of this community, they do refer to its existence. For example, Luke 6 describes Jesus calling together his followers and selecting from that larger group the twelve disciples.

> One of those days Jesus went out to a mountainside to pray, and spent the night praying to God. When morning came, *he called his disciples to him and chose twelve of them*, whom he also designated apostles. (Luke 6:12-13, emphasis added)

We have no indication of the total number of disciples following Jesus, but we do know that it was a group of more than twelve. Don't be surprised if something similar happens in your discipling efforts, and don't underestimate the significance of these "distance learners." You can never really be sure how their lives are being affected.

Groups and one-on-one—Why do both?

One of the mistakes that I often see, especially in organized small-group environments, is that one-on-one discipleship is mostly set aside. Or, if there is any attention given to individuals, it is reactive rather than proactive, implemented only when there is a problem or special need. In my opinion, this is topsy-turvy. Think about it: group leaders often become frustrated because they are generally unable to cultivate a community of disciples who truly love one another or who are willing to open their hearts to one another. The reason for this frustration is that the leader's energies are spent on creating a community through the weekly meeting time rather than individually discipling the group members.

Christian small-group leaders have been trained to build their community through the scarce hours of group time that the members are together, but I argue that the community's environment is a result of the leader's discipling of the members *outside* of the group time. As the orchestra's concert is the consummation of lessons, private practice, and rehearsals, so the group dynamic is the expression of the discipler's individual investment in his disciples. One cannot expect people who have not been discipled to behave like disciples in community.

But when these two dynamics are fused together well, they produce two amazing results: unity and teamwork.

The drawing power of unity

Kevin was an atheist who became friends with our group of disciples in Chicago. When he later became a follower of Jesus, Kevin told us that the group members' love for one another was something he had longed for his whole life. He explained that this made such an impression on him because he had never felt he had a place to belong. Watching people genuinely care for one another, and for him, motivated Kevin to reinvestigate the very claims of Christianity that he had been arguing against and resisting.

I am convinced that unity is the point of engagement with our culture because unity is a high expression of love. The unity of the disciples means that each person has put the advancement of the kingdom of God above his own aggrandizement. *We* replaces *me*. Unity does not mean that everyone should act alike, talk alike, smell alike, and walk alike. That would be the definition of *boring*. No, unity means that every disciple is as concerned about the good of his brother and sister as he is of his own.

Think about it, our unity and love for one another as followers of Christ is a proof to the world that the Father sent Jesus to earth. Jesus prayed for his future disciples: "May they be brought to complete unity to let the world know that you sent me and have loved them even as you have loved me" (John 17:23). Our unity is a proclamation of the gospel. When the world sees our unity, it resonates with them because mankind was not created to live a detached existence but rather to belong.

Unity is at the heart of making disciples because it is rooted in the nature of God. Jesus came to earth to introduce the kingdom of God through demonstrating the unity he experienced with his own Father (see John 14:9-10). He also worked for nearly three years to cultivate unity among his followers, knowing that their relationships with one another would be a picture of the gospel to the world.

So if you're really serious about making disciples, you must also be serious about developing and safeguarding unity. Prepare yourself to help resolve conflicts and train your disciples to be ready to sacrifice their time and resources when God presents your group, or someone in your group, with a need or opportunity.

Robert Bellah sees living in community as an essential component for our own growth and for the benefit of others. He writes, "We find ourselves not independently of other people and institutions but through them. We never get to the bottom of ourselves on our own. We discover who we are face to face and side by side with others in work, love, and learning."[1]

Since adding the community dynamic to discipleship, I've discovered that it has helped defend against individual hypocrisy. Covers are blown and true selves are revealed. The manner in which disciples relate to one another in a group is a strong indication of how each relates to God personally. To know what's really going on inside your disciple, observe how he interacts with other followers of Christ. A person can say he loves God with all his heart and can give a great impression of this being the case, but if he does not relate well with others, he is deceived and/or deceiving (1 John 4:20).

Always remember that disciple-making is not an equipping course on how to do ministry. Disciple-making at its core is learning—and demonstrating—how to relate lovingly to God and others. For this reason you should not despair over conflict and disunity when they come, but rather see them as opportunities to instruct your disciples further on how to love. Conflict in a community of believers is not a disruption to the purpose of God but a chance to express his forgiveness, love, and compassion. Each individual, no matter how difficult he may be at times, is an essential element in building unity. For this reason, be careful not to think, "This could be a good community if only Joe were not on the team." In reality, Joe may be the key to building the unity on the team that God intends.

Teamwork

At the same time I studied the disciple-making methods of Jesus, I also looked more closely at the apostle Paul's approach. Though we often think of Paul as a church planter, in my estimation he was first and foremost a disciple-maker. And what struck me most was that he almost always developed a team.

Many people today attempt to minister alone, but Paul worked with a team throughout his life. In fact, he was constantly on the lookout for disciples to join in his work. In Lystra, Paul met a young disciple named Timothy and recruited him to travel with him, forming a relationship that lasted more than seventeen years.

Two years later Paul came across a married couple named Priscilla and Aquila whom he also taught and equipped. Over thirty years of ministry, Paul had a team of twelve who served with him. I hesitate to call them a traveling team because they would often minister in one location for months or years at a time; yet they did, like Paul, minister in various locations during their lifetime. This team included Jews, Gentiles, a married couple, and a deserter who left Paul after seven years of ministry together. We have no evidence that the twelve were ever together at one time, nor can we be sure that they all had even met one another.

The core of Paul's team was made up of Titus, Timothy, and Luke. Titus was with Paul for nineteen years, while Timothy and Luke were each with him for seventeen years. The rest of the twelve were Aristarchus, Demas, Erastus, Mark, Silas, Trophimus, Tychicus, Priscilla, and Aquila. The average amount of time these team members were associated with Paul was nine and a half years.

As I considered Paul's ministry, I identified four benefits of serving with a team:

1. A team provides spiritual, emotional, and physical help, as well as accountability.
2. A team provides a variety of spiritual gifts. Paul knew his strengths and was aware of his weaknesses. He surrounded himself with men and women who would complement his ministry.
3. A team provides ministry options. Paul was able to send his team members to other cities when a need presented itself.
4. A team provides an opportunity to love and serve others. The interpersonal relationships of the team members demonstrate the good news of Jesus to the world.

When I saw Christianity struggling to grow and flourish in places like Chicago, where I live, even though evangelicals have spent thousands of dollars on advertising, church planting, and outreach with disappointing results, I began to wonder if we were hindered by our methods. Were we fishing solo with rods and reels when we needed to fish as a group with nets?

I could not escape the biblical model: discipleship requires community. Whatever I might learn or accomplish on my own could do very little to advance heavenly causes. My life needed to be synced with other disciples. So our group has taken on yet another dimension: broadening our focus not only to make disciples *within* the group, but striving to make disciples *as* a group. We are now connected in life *and* in purpose. My disciples have become my fellow disciplers.

Adding a Group Approach to Disciple-Making

- Pray for team members. Ask the Lord to lead you to the individuals or couples with whom you can make followers of Jesus.
- Ask: Who would I love being with on a ministry team? Who has a heart and mind like mine about the kingdom of God and ministry?
- Welcome variety in gifting, skills, and personalities. The Holy Spirit gives each person an ability that works in harmony with the other team members.
- Limit the size of your group, and don't try to increase in number too quickly.
- Monitor the spiritual health and maturity of your group members.
- Keep nurturing your one-on-one relationship with each group member.
- Be prepared to launch new groups when your group size becomes too large for you to effectively lead.

Justin's Story, Part 1

In the winter of 2000, Lewie Clark introduced me to discipleship. I had recently become a follower of Jesus; and although I didn't realize it, I desperately wanted guidance. Lewie and I met the previous summer in a Bible study he led, but we had never spent time cultivating our relationship outside of that study time. During my Christmas vacation, Lewie called and scheduled a dinner with me. I remember being a little puzzled at this because we had no apparent reason for meeting. Our ensuing conversation over sandwiches changed the course of my life.

From the moment we sat down together, I could tell Lewie was engaged in our conversation. He didn't look at his food or the floor or other people in the restaurant; he looked at me. He was intent on listening to everything I had to say. His interest was disarming because our conversation wasn't about philosophy or politics or any other topic. The conversation was about *me*. He asked about my dreams, my ambitions, and my relationship with Jesus. He would often pause and think about my answers and ask more questions, probing my statements for their true meaning. He told me things about myself that I had never realized—things he had observed during our study time together and in my interaction with others.

When I got in my car to drive home, I was incredibly excited about being alive and about following Jesus. Looking back I now understand that Lewie had bestowed tremendous value on me through our conversation. He took specific steps to communicate his interest in me, and his interest made me feel incredibly valuable. He asked deep questions, took my answers seriously, pointed out strengths in me that nobody had ever noticed . . . and that was just the first ten minutes! What's more, the ease with which he engaged me was disarming and trust-inspiring. I already respected Lewie a great deal for his wisdom and teaching insight, but after our conversation I admired him for his courage, his authenticity, and his faith. I didn't realize this was to be the first of many such conversations between us.

In the next months and years, Lewie taught me about discipleship—a simple but radical way of life bent on fulfilling Jesus' commission to his followers.

This instruction came through the friendship that he forged with me. Just as Jesus' twelve disciples learned about his kingdom and were prepared to proclaim its arrival by being "with him" (Mark 3:14), so too did I learn by being with Lewie. He spoke truth into my life just as Jesus had done with his disciples, but his exemplary friendship impacted me more profoundly than his words. By being my friend he taught me about friendship, revealing to me what Jesus had revealed to him and thereby fleshing out Jesus' words from John 15:15, "I have called you friends, for everything that I learned from my Father I have made known to you." He encouraged the development of both my heart and mind, displaying to me the radical call of Jesus to live for the glory of God in a thought-provoking and deeply heartfelt way. He bought me biographies of men whose stories stirred my soul. He took me with him to speaking engagements. He introduced me to other disciples. He asked for my prayer and opinions. He nurtured within me an abiding love for the Scriptures. He told me that God had something extraordinary for my future. He didn't tell me what he thought I should do. Instead, he partnered with the Spirit to encourage what Jesus was already doing in my life in order to push me to the next level. He fanned the flame of the Spirit within me. What's more, he was the initiator, the pursuer. Just as Jesus first loved me, so did Lewie.

3

What Is God Like?

I'm often asked to coach people and groups—sometimes entire churches and parachurch organizations—on their disciple-making efforts. Much of the time I come away with the same two feelings: (1) deep appreciation for their intent and (2) disappointment over their approach. Western Christianity seems to be enamored with programs, campaigns, and curricula while giving lesser attention to the heart-and-soul matters of relational connection. If we're not effective, we assume our methodology is what's broken.

At this point many will go back to the basics and reconsider what the Bible teaches about discipleship. Unfortunately, even then the tendency is to skip over the Gospels (Matthew, Mark, Luke, and John) and dive into the book of Acts and Paul's letters. I say this is unfortunate because in bypassing the Gospels we overlook four accounts of the time God came to earth and the great many lessons to be learned from Christ's encounters with seekers, followers, doubters, and grievers. Joseph Hellerman describes it like this:

> The earthly ministry of Jesus of Nazareth constitutes the one time in the history of humanity when heaven fully and finally came to earth. In Matthew, Mark, Luke, and John, we have the opportunity to see the question "What is God like?" answered in the flesh-and-blood

world in which we live. During His incarnation Jesus not only procured our way to heaven. He also shows us how to live on earth. Now we can pattern our lives after Jesus.[1]

What is God like? Asking and answering that question is the starting point of all ministry, discipleship included. In a word, God is *love*.

At the baptism of Jesus, the heavenly Father declared his love for his Son. "And a voice from heaven said, 'This is my Son, whom I love; with him I am well pleased'" (Matthew 3:17). This was a clear declaration of the love bond between the heavenly Father and Jesus. This familial love then became the basis for Jesus' love for his disciples *and* the disciples love for one another. "As the Father has loved me, so have I loved you. Now remain in my love" (John 15:9), and "As I have loved you, so you must love one another. By this all men will know that you are my disciples, if you love one another" (John 13:34-35).

Imitating the methods of Jesus without the family love element will result in a sterile religion rather than a dynamic spiritual family. It is essential for your disciples to understand that God relates to them as a Father and they are to relate to him as sons. This understanding is the basis on which your disciples are to lovingly relate to one another as brothers. The brotherly love your disciples have for one another is a window for the world to see the heavenly Father's love on display. "I in them and you in me. May they be brought to complete unity to let the world know that you sent me and have loved them even as you have loved me" (John 17:23).

Reflecting on the love bond she was forming with her soon-to-be husband, Anne Morrow Lindbergh wrote:

> To be deeply in love is, of course, a great liberating force and the most common experience that frees . . . The sheer fact of finding myself loved was unbelievable and changed my world, my feelings about life and myself. I was given confidence, strength, and almost a new

character. The man I was to marry believed in me and
what I could do, and consequently I found I could do
more than I realized.[2]

Mrs. Lindbergh was of course writing about romantic love, but
her observations are true of familial love as well. Love liberates, heals,
and empowers. And everyone wants to be loved. Just ask Solomon:
"What a man desires is unfailing love" (Proverbs 19:22)—and even
Forrest Gump: "I am not a smart man, but I know what love is."[3]

There is only one way and there will always be only one way to
make disciples, and that is to love. It's as if every man and woman
wears a sign that reads: *To understand my behavior, recognize my need
to be loved.* Discipleship at its core is demonstrating how to love.

Teaching your disciples how to love

Love marks the follower of Jesus, yet for many love does not come
easily. It is therefore vital in the training of your disciples that
you demonstrate not only how to express love, but also how to
receive it.

Recently I was with one of our groups of disciples and in my
private conversations I was impressed with the love each one had
for the others. I assumed they all knew of this mutual respect, but
I later learned that none of them had expressed their love because
embarrassment had closed off their heartfelt affection. Immediately
I went to each person and gave them the assignment of meeting
face-to-face with each of the other group members to express their
love directly and intentionally.

Love is meant to be communicated, yet this can be awkward
for those who do not have an expressive type of personality, did
not grow up in an affectionate family, or have been hurt so badly
that they've walled off their emotions. I believe that the ease of
giving and receiving affection can be a spiritual indicator in the life
of a disciple. Any awkwardness with affection could be masking a
deeper issue or hint at interpersonal tension. It's difficult for people
to be affectionate when they're at odds.

Ideas that might help you create an atmosphere of love with your disciples include:

- Encourage your disciples to express specific reasons why they love and value another person, something more than a simple (and perhaps meaningless) "I love you, man!"
- Coach your disciples to look for opportunities to serve others in the group. Nothing says "I love you" like meeting a need.
- Discuss with your disciples the strengths of others, and then encourage them to express their appreciation for those strengths to those individuals. It's easy and natural to see the weaknesses of others, which often blinds us to their strengths.
- Read the book *The Heart of the Five Love Languages* by Gary Chapman for a better understanding of the various ways love can be demonstrated.
- Include individual attention by having each of your disciples get together one-on-one for the purpose of sharing their life stories with each other.

Let me just add a few thoughts about physical affection. Some are not comfortable with this kind of display, but it is quite biblical. In my opinion, not only is physical affection necessary between the discipler and his disciple, it is also important for your disciples to be affectionate with one another. Just as affection is a natural expression of love in a healthy family, so it should be among the children of God.

Luke's writing gives us a glimpse into the freedom that people had in expressing their affection to the apostle Paul. "When he [Paul] had said this, he knelt down with all of them and prayed. They all wept as they embraced him and kissed him" (Acts 20:36-37). Although our culture is generally uncomfortable with expressing affection with a kiss, I do believe we should go beyond handshakes, high-fives, and fist bumps. Not that these are all empty expressions, but we're not strangers meeting for the first time, and we have much more to celebrate than a BCS championship. We are members of an eternal family whose hallmark is love. Let's show it.

The discipler: an intercessor and cheerleader

The love expressed to another person is really only as valuable as the authenticity of the love. If it is in word only, it may not be love at all. So I would say to all who are serious about investing themselves in disciple-making, be sure your love is the real thing. Don't fake it.

And one sure way to enrich your love for your disciples is to pray for them.

My dad has prayed for me every day for more than fifty years. I simply cannot describe the security and love that I feel each time he says to me, "Son, I pray for you every day."

Prayer is a gift of love for you to give to your disciple. Telling your disciple that you pray for him is just another way of saying "I love you." You may not have money, possessions, or position, but anyone can give the gift of prayer.

Both Jesus and Paul give us the example of a discipler praying for his disciples. Jesus prayed for his disciples throughout his ministry, and we even have one of those prayers recorded for us in John 17. Paul not only consistently prays for his disciples, but he also regularly *told* them that he was praying for them and even gave them the content of those prayers (e.g., Ephesians 1:15-23). I know of no better way of loving your disciple than to daily offer up prayers on his behalf.

Here are a couple of suggestions:

- Use the prayers of Paul and pray them for your disciple: "I keep asking that the God of our Lord Jesus Christ, the glorious Father, may give _____ the Spirit of wisdom and revelation, so that _____ may know him better" (Ephesians 1:17).
- Periodically send a text message or email to your disciple to let him know that you prayed for him that morning.

- Keep pictures of your disciples in a 3x5 box and rotate the pictures as a prayer reminder.

Another love-builder is to be your disciple's cheerleader. The apostle Paul was not only affectionate but also enthusiastic toward his disciples. He understood that every son and daughter has been created by God for an eternal purpose. As a discipler, I seek to join the Holy Spirit to find and fulfill that purpose for my disciple. No matter how dire the circumstances in a person's life, I must never lose confidence in the hope that God is at work in that individual and that Jesus will carry it on to completion.

Love should be expressed enthusiastically, assuring your disciple that he brings pleasure to your life and to the lives of others. Listen again to Paul: "We loved you so much that we were delighted to share with you not only the gospel of God but our lives as well, because you had become so dear to us" (1 Thessalonians 2:8). These are not halfhearted words from a numb soul; they are expressive and real. And they renew the heart of the listening disciple.

By expressing love we also express value. Again, Paul placed great value on the Christ-followers he discipled. One would walk away from Paul's presence with a sense of purpose and significance. Listen as he unashamedly expresses joy and gratitude for the disciples at Thessalonica: "For what is our hope, our joy, or the crown in which we will glory in the presence of our Lord Jesus when he comes? Is it not you? Indeed, you are our glory and joy" (1 Thessalonians 2:19-20).

I have never had any Christian leader express to me that I was their "glory or joy." Nor has anyone come to me and expressed their gratitude to God for me as Paul did to his disciples: "How can we thank God enough for you in return for all the joy we have in the presence of our God because of you?" (1 Thessalonians 3:9). But after reading this passage, I couldn't get on the phone fast enough to express my love and gratitude to those people I had discipled over the years. I had been given permission to be extravagant in my love.

Love is just an abstract thought when we only talk about it. But we certainly recognize it when it's set in motion through expression.

Love *in deed*, and you will make disciples.

Justin's Story, Part 2

During our first dinner together, Lewie asked me about my dreams. I told him that I considered proclaiming Christ in a foreign country. He immediately began exploring the idea with me. Before dinner was over, he told me of an opportunity to be a "journeyman" missionary with an organization called the International Mission Board. A few weeks later I received a package in the mail with the details of how to put my dream into motion—a package that Lewie had requested on my behalf.

A few months later Lewie was in Brazil with some other elders from our church. While he was there he took the initiative to sit down with an American missionary working in the city of São Paulo and asked him, "What if I could send you a young man who could make disciples?" Danny, the missionary, was reluctant at first because he felt a journeyman would need a fair amount of supervision, yet Lewie explained to Danny the vision of discipleship he had shared with me and the potential he saw in me to carry it out. Danny soon agreed to create a new missionary position for me to come and fill. When Lewie returned back to the States and shared this with me, I was stunned. Other than Jesus himself, no one had ever been such an advocate for me. I cannot express the love and empowerment I received through that experience.

Practically speaking, Lewie's approach to discipleship was anchored by questions that he used like keys to unlock my thoughts. No question was asked more frequently and with more genuine interest than, *Why?* As Lewie joined the Spirit in molding me to Jesus' image, we discussed many grace-covered areas of sin in my life. He took my sin very seriously, but he never tried to convince me that my sin was sinful. He didn't remind me how bad it was in order to motivate me not to do it anymore, which was how sin in my life had normally been treated. Rather, he explored with me *why* I chose to disobey. By God's Spirit, I already knew my sin was sinful. I already understood the gravity of its destructive power, but at that time I rarely understood my deep motivation for sinning. The overly simple explanation of, "I am just a sinner, I am depraved," wasn't adequate. He showed me how to dig into my thoughts and feelings and find the snowball that caused the avalanche (e.g., disappointment, frustration with God, loneliness). He provided me with the spiritual, mental, and emotional wherewithal to understand and be honest about my deepest motivations—to not just understand *what* my sin was but *why* I was sinning.

We discussed Scripture, but even then, he didn't quote it to me as if that would magically solve the problem, nor did he simply say, "Believe the promises of God." His unassuming questions helped me realize how much he wanted to *understand* me and my problems, not just to give me advice or artificially smooth things over with scripturally proof-texted platitudes. He wished to provide a context of healing where I would experience the cross-centered love of Jesus. He entered into the pain with me. He empathized. He got as close as possible to actually bearing my pain, and he demonstrated his own belief in the promises of God. Through his instruction I learned not just *what* to believe but *how* to believe it.

Before my relationship with Lewie, no one had ever modeled for me, in a relational way, what it meant to be a follower of Jesus. By "in a relational way," I mean that nobody ever established a relationship with me where the *relationship itself*, the dynamic between us, was the facilitating avenue through which I learned what it meant to be like Jesus. Nobody came alongside me, got to know me, asked me about my life and my dreams, listened to me, helped me face my fears and insecurities, shared my struggles and joys as if they were their own, and peered deeply into the Scriptures in an effort to answer tough questions and cultivate a profound love for truth. I had listened to countless sermons, witnessed other Christians on Sundays, attended Sunday school, and participated in a youth group, but I was always left with a nagging feeling that there was something more, something that I was missing. My relationship with Lewie changed that. I saw in Lewie a rich, authentic love for Jesus. The way he talked about Jesus was beautiful. I could tell they were best friends. The way he lived for him was compelling. Amazingly enough, transferring his own zeal for Christ to me was the most loving thing he (or anyone else) could do. In the end, I began realizing that for so many years I was missing authentic love.

4

That's Where I Belong

The Sound of Music is one of my favorite movies, and Captain von Trapp is my favorite character. I'm entertained by the absurd way he tries to lead his family, an obvious carryover from his discipline as an officer in the navy. But his actions amuse me only because I know that sometime in act 2 he'll come to his senses and become more of a dad and less of a captain. After all, children aren't recruits and a family is not a company, military or otherwise.

Although the captain loves his children and the children love him, his organizational structure raises unnatural barriers between them. Their relationship is lost, hidden behind the formalities of doing things "just so." It isn't until the von Trapps learn to act like a family that smiles, laughter, and respect return to their home and fear and intimidation run away.

The nature of a family is unlike any other organization. Some organizations operate better than others—this is true of families as well—but we do not have the same hopes and expectations of organizations as we do of families. Families are truly people-centered environments of love, acceptance, forgiveness, support, honesty, and nurture. At least the healthy ones are. By nature of what they're created to accomplish, families have more heart and soul to them than organizations do. Even the most respected of organizations—whether a branch of the military, an office of the government, a nonprofit humanitarian outreach, or even an evangelical mission—is structured in such a way that a person can be demoted or lose employment or membership due to misbehavior or rule-breaking, but a family member will always belong.

Interestingly, the apostle Paul presents the church (*ekklesia*) as the "family" or "household" of God (see 1 Timothy 3:14-15), yet our Western-minded approach to church is often to see it as an organization instead. We labor over church constitutions, by-laws, and forms of church government, and then institute programs to keep the church running on the tracks we've laid. And while I'm not saying that these things are entirely unnecessary, they do tend to be much more organizational than relational, and are extemporaneous to the family. I believe this is a fundamental reason why many churches have no more success at disciple-making than Captain von Trapp had at winning the hearts of his children. First and foremost, people need to know—*really* know—that they belong.

In Philippians 2:22 we get a glimpse into Paul's approach to disciple-making where he writes of the father-son connection between himself and Timothy (again a family relationship). Disciples are best made in the context of a spiritual family. As long as we ignore this fact and choose instead to anchor our disciple-making in programs, we will frustrate the discipler and the disciple. There is a marked difference between how an organization develops its people and how a parent loves his child.

Disciple-makers will get it wrong if they try to reform a person's character by concentrating on outward conformity to others' expectations. C. S. Lewis wrote, "You can't get second things by putting them first. You get second things only by putting first things first."[1] I believe that discipleship must begin by engrafting a person into a group (family) where he feels that he truly belongs, and out of that belonging will flow the spiritual formation of his life and character. Belonging is the first thing.

First things

Steve was a handsome, athletic, musically talented, and outgoing college student. But he was having some personal struggles and asked if I would start meeting with him on a regular basis. I thoroughly enjoyed getting to know Steve. After nearly a year of conversations, however, I still felt as if something was going on inside him that he hadn't been willing to address. Whatever it was kept Steve locked up; we talked about the same issues over and over, and he was stuck on the same problems. Good talks, but little progress.

When a person is suffocating—usually because of fear—it may take months for their emotional oxygen level to normalize, and only then can they unburden themselves of what has been pressing down on them. A person who is afraid would rather lie (even as a believer) than be forced to tell you his greatest shame or fear.

One day, seemingly out of the blue, Steve finally uncorked the bottle of his emotions and told me the heartbreaking story of his childhood home life. In short: Steve's mom had an affair, then later when his father died in an on-the-job accident, the man with whom his mom was having the affair moved in with Steve and his mom while still married to his wife. Steve said he was afraid that if I found out about his home life I would not continue to be his friend.

During the same time frame that I had been meeting with Steve, I had begun the practice of pulling together all the men I was discipling into a weekly group meeting. Steve was part of the group, and it was soon evident that he was benefitting from the camaraderie. But when he told me about his home situation, he also asked if I thought he should tell the other guys in the group. Steve's shame had taken such deep root, he was convinced that he was damaged and unwanted goods. He was sure that the other guys would no longer want him around. Steve's thinking reminded me of something that my friend, Brian, had once said when wrestling through some of his own problems: "There are things that I don't want to deal with alone, but I also don't want to take anyone there with me."

The next time we met, I had Steve tell his story to the group. I'd like to say that the guys all rushed to reassure him, but they didn't.

Instead, there was only silence. Awkward silence. Letting this newfound transparency sink in for a minute, I finally said, "Okay, Steve has just shared with us one of the most difficult things in his life. What do you need to say to him?" One guy told Steve that he loved him. Another got up, walked across the room and gave Steve a hug. Someone else said that this information did not change how he felt about Steve.

We all experienced something that day—what it means to belong. Our past does not disqualify us. Our shame does not remove us. Healing begins with honesty. Honesty begins with trust. And trust begins with belonging. This is the gospel-like nature of disciple-making and why it can never be distanced from the cross. Jesus gave his life for the salvation of any who would believe in him. There is no prequalification process, no exclusivity clause. Steve's honesty reminded us of that.

Again, as Lewis says, "You can't get second things by putting them first." It is fruitless to try to get your disciples to live by kingdom values or to have right attitudes if they do not understand to whom they belong. You will become frustrated and you will frustrate your disciples if you do not begin by helping them unite to God and to other disciples.

I simply cannot say enough about the importance of belonging. Even the most introverted people long to be attached to others in ways that are loving, accepting, and nurturing. This basic need explains why, when your disciple feels disconnected, his behavior will often become erratic and sometimes self-destructive. As he tries to compensate for his detachment, your disciple may enter into inappropriate and/or dysfunctional relationships that offer the illusion that he belongs. But these relationships will not move him forward spiritually and will eventually become an obstacle to be overcome.

Belonging is revolutionary. And to many people, especially those who have been through the deep waters of neglect, abandonment, and abuse, your reaching out to them will be the first signal of love they have seen in a very long time.

Who loves you?

Chicago Tribune writer Marla Paul wrote a self-revealing column where she confessed sadness and frustration over her inability to build and sustain friendships. She ended with: "Sometimes it seems easier to just give up and accept disconnectedness as a dark and unshakable companion; but, that's not the companion I want."[2]

To her surprise, Ms. Paul was inundated with letters from readers who admitted they were experiencing the same kind of isolation she had described. One person wrote, "I've often felt that I'm standing outside looking through the window of a party to which I was not invited."

Part of the discipling process is helping your disciple understand that he belongs to God as a son and to the rest of God's family as a brother (see Hebrews 2:11). When Jesus called his men to follow him, he was also calling them to belong to one another. Jesus formed a community because it flowed out of his nature to do so (he was one with the Father and with the Holy Spirit) and because he knew that for his disciples to live as God intended, they must form strong bonds of love.

Since I have come to understand more about the necessity of belonging, I have rarely attempted to disciple anyone apart from their being in a community of other disciples. A significant part of the disciple's life is in learning to both give and receive love. How can this be accomplished if a person has no relationships on the line, ones that will be enriched when love is in place or that will shrivel if it is not? No, love cannot be learned in theory. A disciple is not a loner. He belongs.

I guess it is obvious then that starting a discipling community is much more challenging than starting a typical Bible study or small group. It often takes months and years for a group to solidify, but the process does become easier as your disciples learn how to love one another. And the outcome is so beautiful to watch; there really is no end in sight to what God can do through a community of connected Christ-followers.

What better place?

In all this discussion about the family-like nature of good discipler-to-disciple relationships, let's not overlook the opportunity that God presents parents to disciple their children. In fact, I believe that the Christian home is a literal breeding ground for Christ-followers. Good parents create an environment that is not only safe for the child but also moves the child onto maturity. And while parents understand that the maturing process takes time, it comes with the expectation that someday their children will leave home to raise their own families, taking with them a vibrant relationship with Christ and the know-how of discipleship. One can only imagine the expansion of the kingdom of God if parents held the spiritual development of their children as a high priority.

When the apostle Paul was looking for men to lead the church, he looked for men who were good husbands and dads. He wrote, "If anyone does not know how to manage his own family, how can he take care of God's church?" (1 Timothy 3:5). Paul understood the family essence of the church and that the same principles required to build a healthy family are the same values that will multiply the kingdom of God. The types of leaders that are necessary to begin and sustain a multiplication of the kingdom of God are godly moms and dads. The instruction, encouragement, kindness, time, and sacrificial love that go into raising godly children are the same necessary ingredients to make followers of Jesus. Paul revealed his own parental approach to disciple-making when he wrote: "For you know that we dealt with each of you as a father deals with his own children, encouraging, comforting and urging you to live lives worthy of God, who calls you into his kingdom and glory" (1 Thessalonians 2:11-12).

Sadly, the same parents who have raised godly children often feel inadequate to make disciples of Jesus because Christianity has turned discipling into an educational method through curriculum, classrooms, and certification rather than a family relationship. Could it be that the church is passing over highly qualified and experienced kingdom leaders because they are not perceived as "qualified"? Somehow, I think Paul and other vintage New Testament leaders would encourage us to adjust our thinking.

My growing family

Family has always been important to me. My parents raised my siblings and me—I have three sisters and three brothers—to care about one another. Sure, we've had our disagreements and squabbles, but for the most part we've remained closely connected over the years and miles. I've been fortunate that way. But I've also been blessed to see my "family" grow as God has continued to add friends to my life—something that rocketed to the top of my things-to-be-thankful-for list a few years ago when I was diagnosed with prostate cancer.

I remember the doctor's words and expression as if it happened just a few days ago: "Unfortunately, Mr. Clark, you do have cancer and the levels are concerning. I recommend surgery as soon as possible." And so, two months later I found myself waking up to the obnoxious alarm of an IV pump in Northwestern Memorial Hospital.

When the surgeon came in to check on me the next morning, he asked, "Who are you?"

I was puzzled by his question, and thought to myself, *You just operated on me yesterday, and we were up close and personal even if I was asleep the whole time. I hope you can at least remember who I am!*

Perhaps sensing that I was confused by his question, he explained that after surgery, when he went to the waiting room and asked to talk to the Clark family, a group of white, black, Asian, young, and old people all stood up and walked toward him. One older gentleman had spoken for the group and said, "Yes, we're the Clark family. We're a different kind of family, but we're Lewie's family."

Then the doctor repeated his question, "Who are you?"

At that moment I was flooded with a sense of belonging. I had known that God was watching over me during my illness, but it brought such added relief to know that he had also surrounded me with a group of people who had taken my burden as their own.

The idea of family may send chills down your spine because of a painful past, or it may bring bright memories of comfort and safety. Either way, God has placed you in a new kind of family whose future is secure and whose love is unending. What an honor we've been given to invite others into this family.

Chris's Story

Although I was raised in a household of faith and knew the Christian religion well, it wasn't until the age of twenty-three that love became the issue for me. Not wanting for anything, and being faithful to my religion, I still was unsatisfied.

I had known Lewie Clark as the singles pastor at my church and had met with him on several occasions—some of my life's defining moments. What was interesting to me was that he didn't try to solve and provide the answers to my life questions. Instead he sought out my passions and my heart while conveying that I had value and that I was loved by God—whom I only seemed to know as a distant authority figure. My interest was piqued and I was thirsty.

Being "scared straight" hadn't worked for me, but Lewie communicated that he and God were genuinely interested in me. Due to his friendship, love, and commitment to seeing me grow as a follower of Jesus, I experienced an understanding of God's love and ultimately how my self-righteousness had kept me from playing my role in the building of the kingdom.

Over the next several years a small community of Jesus-followers grew. Lewie showed us hospitality by giving us his personal space and demonstrated the importance of loving one another. Today, the men in that original community are impacting the kingdom in ways we could not have imagined. In a few years' time, many lost individuals have been united into God's family and have found power in the sacrificial love they've experienced through a community of disciples.

This overpowering desire for someone to fill his or her void with love has consumed my wife and me. The sacrifice of giving through hospitality and love is not easy, but it is small compared to the gift we've received. We must be intentional to open our home and lives to anyone interested and hope Jesus will use us our gifts to impact his kingdom.

Over the past six years the Father has used us as instruments in the lives of individuals and families seeking to fill the void. By the world's standards, we're not special, we're not trained, just blessed by God who loves us.

5

Hospitality

How does healing take place? Many words, such as
care and compassion, understanding and forgiveness,
fellowship and community, have been used for the
healing task of the Christian minister. I like to use
the word hospitality, not only because it has such
deep roots in the Judaeo-Christian tradition, but also,
and primarily, because it gives us more insight into
the nature of response to the human condition of
loneliness. Hospitality is the virtue which allows us to
break through the narrowness of our own fears and to
open our houses to the stranger, with the intuition that
salvation comes to us in the form of a tired traveler.
Hospitality makes anxious disciples into powerful
witnesses, makes suspicious owners into generous givers
and makes closed-minded sectarians into interested
recipients of new ideas and insights.
—Henri Nouwen

I lived for ten years in the same apartment, and during that entire
time I entertained only six overnight guests and no dinner guests.
I conducted all "ministry" outside the walls of my home. *That has*

changed. Drastically. Over the past five years I've had nearly one thousand overnight guests and too many dinner guests to count. I didn't back into this change. It was intentional.

On the last church staff where I served, we studied through the qualifications of an elder—some Bible translations call it "overseer"—in 1 Timothy 3 and Titus 1. Even though I'd read and studied these passages numerous times, something I hadn't noticed before stood out to me on this occasion: "The overseer must be . . . *hospitable*" (1 Timothy 3:2, emphasis added). I can't explain why this had never really caught my attention, but I suspect if you were to ask a hundred Christians to list the things that qualify a person for leadership in the church, very few, if any, would think to mention hospitality. Yet here it is on God's list, given equal billing to "above reproach," "able to teach," "not given to drunkenness," and "not violent."

Evidently, hospitality is very important to God.

With this revelation fresh on my mind and heart, I set out to make hospitality a part of my life. First on my to-do list: learn to cook.

Now, learning to cook means different things to different people. To some it means learning basics, like the difference between boiling and broiling. To others who are more advanced it means learning to discriminate between dill seed and dill weed. (Confession: I didn't know either. I had to look it up.) I was definitely in the beginners' class. Up to this point in time I had never used my oven. Well, to be perfectly honest, I had *used* my oven, but not *as* an oven.

You see, one day a neighbor lady knocked on my door. She explained that she had been baking a birthday cake and her oven had quit working before the cake was done. She then asked if she could finish it in mine. I invited her in, led her to the kitchen, and then—a bit sheepishly—emptied all the books out of my oven so she could turn it on and use it for its intended purpose. Until that day my oven had been a book cabinet!

But not anymore.

Hospitality, and more particularly, enjoying a meal together—which often includes preparing the meal together—has become an integral part of my disciple-making endeavors. This is more than a method or strategy, it is something that I believe expresses the heart and nature of God and carries on the ministry of Christ, as the following quotes suggest.

> "Luke [writer of the gospel] portrays Jesus not only as a guest at the table of others, but also as an indiscriminate host who welcomes those outside the boundaries of religious and social approval."[1]

> "Jesus used hospitality to connect to the poor, the wealthy, the working man and the disenfranchised in order for them to become his followers."[2]

Just as Jesus used hospitality to make himself available to people, so we can use it as a means of connecting—and staying connected—to our disciples. This provides us with opportunities to serve our disciples and to carve out a place for them to belong. Serving and disciple-making are inseparable. Remember what Jesus said:

> "You know that those who are regarded as rulers of the Gentiles lord it over them, and their high officials exercise authority over them. Not so with you. Instead, whoever wants to become great among you must be your servant, and whoever wants to be first must be slave of all. For even the Son of Man did not come to be served, but to serve, and to give his life as a ransom for many." (Mark 10:42-45)

Being hospitable puts us in the role of serving others and meeting their needs. Sounds Jesus-like, doesn't it?

Hospitality, front and center

I'm often asked, "What does your ministry look like?" or "What do you do?" My general response is, "Come and see for yourself," because it is much easier to understand by experience than by explanation. Still, if I'm pushed to give an answer, I say that we primarily reach out to people through hospitality. If we must name a key method—for evangelism and discipleship—hospitality is it.

Each week our discipling community here in Chicago enjoys a meal together. Yes, a lot of one-to-one relational ministry goes on at other times, but we try to reserve one evening each week—usually Tuesday—as a time for us all to be together. This is very much a family dinner. Setting the table, enjoying great conversation (sometimes planned and sometimes spontaneous), and cleaning up takes an entire evening. I'm always a little let down when the last guest leaves.

When a new person joins our community, we give the entire mealtime to him or her to share their story. This is a great way to get to know them, and they to know us. Judy said, "It was powerful to have people so intently listen to my story. I knew they were listening because they asked questions, and their questions demonstrated that they wanted to know even more about me."

We often have visitors at our table too. Recently we hosted six students from Virginia Tech who had come to see firsthand what a disciple-making community looks like in an urban setting. They were all southern and we were all northern, so we had to explain why we didn't have sugar in our iced tea, and they had to overcome the shock of learning that some people have never eaten catfish!

One evening a guy named Brent joined us. He was an unexpected guest. I don't remember what the topic of conversation was, but somewhere during the course of the meal Brent spoke up. He said, "I really don't know you people, but for some reason I trust you and I want to ask a favor. My parent's marriage is in trouble and I have a younger brother and sister still at home, and I just don't know what to do. Would you please pray for us?" Brent's request set the course for the rest of the evening. Any plan was thrown out the window as we realized the Lord had brought Brent to us for a reason. We asked him to tell us more of the story, and we then spent time in prayer for Brent and his family. Hospitality not only allows people to be open, but it sets a safe environment so the weary can find rest, hope, and refreshment.

Think of it this way: Disciples are *children* of God, therefore a home is the ideal environment for a disciple to experience the parental nature of God, what it means to belong to a family, how to love and serve others, and how to attach to brothers and sisters.

While we're on this topic, I want to emphasize again to moms and dads that your home—your family life—is also the most ideal means by which to disciple your own children. Sons and daughters can witness what it means to follow Jesus by observing the daily lives of their parents and to watch them respond when the routine is interrupted. Many parents seem to scoot their children to the side when the family faces significant decisions or challenges. I understand that this is sometimes necessary, but I also think such times and circumstances present rich opportunities for training children in drawing near to the Savior. Please don't miss these teachable moments.

Hospitality or entertainment?

We tend to compartmentalize, often separating our ministry life from our home life. Even when ministry is conducted "in the home," we think of it as a warm or convenient venue, a meeting place rather than a family gathering. But I'm out to challenge that notion and to change it wherever I can. Our homes, no matter how big or how small, can be—and I believe should be—our base of ministry.

I do understand that hospitality can sound a little threatening. Many people are not accustomed to having guests in their home and may need help in overcoming some fears and insecurities on the front end. My friend, Rachel Haynes, who works in the hospitality industry, has taught me a great deal about the differences between *entertainment* and *hospitality*. This has helped change my perspective and build my confidence. I share some of these contrasts here, hoping that you will find them as helpful as I have.

- Entertainment is host-centered; he or she determines the setting and agenda. Hospitality is guest-centered; their needs and comfort are priority.
- Entertainment is meant to impress the guests. Hospitality strives to empower them.
- Entertainment hosts guests. Hospitality serves them.
- Entertainment showcases houses and décor. Hospitality demonstrates love and honor.
- Entertainment is based on a budget. Hospitality is based on generosity.
- Entertainment is exclusive; some belong and others do not. Hospitality is inclusive; all are welcome.
- Entertainment is something we *do*. Hospitality expresses who we *are*.

As the Father, Son, and Holy Spirit opened up their family at a great sacrifice, allowing us to be adopted as children of God, so we can open up our homes to give an experiential demonstration of the love of God to others. It will take time and money, but the love behind those costs sets up hospitality as an illustration of the gospel.

The Benefits of Hospitality to Disciple-Making

- Hospitality provides an opportunity to serve your disciple. Serving is another way to say "I love you."
- Hospitality opens up your life to your disciple. A home is a personal and intimate space.
- Hospitality provides your disciple an opportunity to observe how you relate to your wife and children.
- Hospitality provides an opportunity for your children to serve others and to learn how to share.
- Hospitality provides an opportunity for your children to love others and for others to love your children.
- Hospitality provides a place for your disciple to belong.

- Hospitality provides a place for your disciple to serve by helping with preparation, cleanup, and caring for other guests.
- Hospitality provides an opportunity for you to observe how your disciple relates to others.

Planning for the unplanned

To have a heart of hospitality means to be prepared for surprises and unexpected guests, and to accept that these are not disruptions but appointments from God. I wish I could say that I'm spring-loaded to being hospitable every hour of every day, but even though I've witnessed many times the beauty of hearts being turned toward Christ in such settings, sometimes I'm not very motivated.

The winter of 2011 was harsh, even by Chicago standards. After one particular blizzard (I'm not exaggerating by using that word), cars were literally buried beneath the snow. Once we were able to get to our cars—almost two full days after the snow stopped—it took hours to dig them out. If you've ever shoveled that much snow, you know what I mean when I say that I was exhausted. It was all I could do to carry myself back inside my apartment, where heat, an easy chair, and a cup of hot chocolate were soon to be mine. The spoils of victory!

Then my phone rang. A friend was calling to explain that he and his fiancée were stranded at O'Hare International Airport, and he wanted to know if they could spend the night with me. This meant, of course, that I would need to jump in my recently resurrected car and make the slippery trek to the airport. My body said no, but my heart said yes. And it's always best to listen to one's heart in these situations.

Because I often have a roommate or two (who generally share the heart of hospitality), I sometimes wake up to discover that strangers (strangers to me, anyway) have spent the night. One particular morning I walked down the hallway and saw out of the corner of my eye a young man sitting on the edge of the bathtub—fully clothed, thankfully, but looking confused. I quickly introduced myself (hoping he was not a serial killer), and Daniel then told me that he was from India and had arrived in the U.S. the night before to meet his girlfriend's family. He had gotten up that morning wanting to take a shower, but this being his first time in our country, he couldn't figure out how to make the faucet work. We've been friends now for a few years and still laugh about our first encounter.

Sometimes the surprise has gone the other way, when God has presented discipling opportunities by *preventing* the expected guests from showing up. One evening I had prepared a roast dinner complete with potatoes, carrots, onions, gravy, French bread, and dessert (my oven was no longer a bookcase). Usually we have 8-12 people at dinner, but on this particular night a collision of circumstances kept everyone away except one. Only Leah showed up that night.

Sensing her embarrassment, I told Leah not to feel bad about the work I had put into the preparation because I saw the dinner as an appointment from God. The Lord knew that she and I needed for just the two of us to spend time together. The timing was perfect. The conversation would not have been as meaningful if it had occurred two weeks earlier or two weeks later. That evening cemented our relationship as we had time to talk through many topics without interruption. Rather than being disappointed in the ten who did not show up, I rejoiced in the opportunity to spend time with the one who did. Needless to say we had plenty to eat and fewer dishes to clean!

For all the work that hospitality may seem to require on the front end, I assure you that it gives more than it takes. That is true of most things I could say about discipleship, or any service we may perform in the name of Christ. Turns out, hospitality is contagious. Maybe that's why God wants us to practice it.

Jamie's Story

My encounter with a discipling community came shortly after graduating from a conservative Christian college. While the knowledge I gained about the Bible and learning to think biblically was invaluable, my relationship with my professors really shaped my experience there. One relationship in particular with my advisor, Lewie, really started me on a journey of encountering the person of Christ. At the time I thought I was just going deeper in my walk with God, but in retrospect it began a process of understanding the person of God and therefore developing more of a relationship with him.

Joining this group was a continuation of what God had started in my friendship with my advisor. I remember after one of the first conversations with Lewie, walking away and asking myself, "Do I really know what it means to be a disciple?" This word is so familiar in our Christian lingo, but leaves much to be understood as far as how it is lived out in day-to-day life.

That year in Chicago was one of the hardest years of my life. Being fresh out of college, many of my dreams and aspirations were shaken by some harsher realities of life. Relationships that had been formational throughout my years experienced turbulent curves. I came to the end of myself. I finally realized that though I had worked my whole life at being a "goody-goody," this was not, in fact, righteousness. God's love for me was not based on my merit. As those pillars came crashing down, I needed to be loved. And I was.

That's what my discipling community—my family in Chicago—provided. I can't count the number of times I heard "'Disciple,' in a word, is love." Love was what I encountered. Love was what brought healing. It happened around a dinner table. It happened sitting down in conversation sipping on tea. At times it was an awkward dance as I learned to accept the love of the other people sitting around the table with me and learned how to show them love. But it happened.

I have much to learn about what it means to disciple, but I have at least learned the importance of it and have tasted how love goes hand-in-hand with showing others what it means to follow Christ.

We are the family of God and we seek to live that way.

Toussaint and Khalid were the first people we connected with when we came to Chicago and they are still with us today. The Lord has bonded our hearts with a unity of purpose and friendship.

Ryan Seibert joined me in Chicago to help advance the kingdom through making disciples of Jesus. He's been a trooper as we launched by faith into unchartered waters. Here he is pictured with his wife Josi.

During our first year in Chicago, Jeremy (left) caught the vision of disciple-making and he and his wife, Julia, have never turned back. Here he is pictured at our Christmas party with two of his disciples: Sean (center), who now disciples college students in Chicago, and Louie (right) who, along with his wife, Ellie, makes disciples in Alaska.

Table fellowship was a powerful symbol in Jesus' disciple-making ministry. Our weekly meals are not only a time to enjoy each other's company, they are also a reminder of the Father's inviting love and an avenue through which a group of disciples learns to love one another.

The Lord's Supper is a regular event at our meals together. When celebrated in a small group of disciples, it gives us the opportunity to speak God's forgiveness and love to each other as we pass the elements around the table.

You don't need anything fancy to have a welcoming place that feels like home, even an urban apartment will do (we occupy the top two apartments). Each year we've hosted over 200 overnight guests and hundreds of dinner guests.

I love the sight of shoes at the door. Each pair represents a person to serve and love.

Each year college students from around the country visit us to learn about making disciples of Jesus. Here I am addressing a group from Clemson University.

Another college group, this one from the University of Central Arkansas.

Danny Jones (standing, center) is one of the first people I discipled (over 30 years ago). He now has disciples all over the U.S. and Eastern Europe. Standing to Danny's right is Peter, one of his disciples from Slovakia.

6

The Discipleship Relationship

Taylor Gardner discipled me and trained me—not just *taught* me—to be a follower of Jesus Christ. I wish you could meet him; his spirit is contagious. Even now, at an age when most people would have been relaxing in retirement, Taylor is going strong in the Dallas metroplex serving the people of Stonebriar Community Church through pastoral care. For as long as I have known him, Taylor's life has displayed an unbroken commitment to discipleship.

Of the many things that I learned from Taylor, his life stands out as an illustration of a servant's heart. I recall an incident that occurred more than thirty years ago. I was living in Kansas City at the time where I was a senior at Calvary Bible College and he was the dean of students. One evening I received the news that my dad had been severely injured in a motorcycle accident in Indiana, hundreds of miles away. I felt so distant and so alone, and if I'm honest, more than a little afraid. And who do you think showed up at my doorstep? Taylor Gardner, of course. Though it was late and he lived on the other side of the city, Taylor came to sit with me and to make sure I was all right.

I'll never forget that act of kindness as long as I live.

Another great contribution that Taylor gave me was simply this: he believed in me. I cannot emphasize the importance of this enough in the discipler-disciple relationship. You must infuse your disciple with the assurance that you believe in him—that you know he can and will be a world-changer; that he will, by the grace of God, discover, embrace, and fulfill his purpose. Taylor Gardner, and my dad, gave me that.

Believing in someone requires one act of love after another. And that love must be expressed in attitudes like patience and encouragement through words of affirmation and reassurance as you empower your disciple to persevere. He will often want to quit and sometimes not even want to start. At any given moment in the relationship, you will be coach, cheerleader, and trainer. And sometimes all three.

Taylor helped by opening up ministry opportunities for me, even when he knew he could have done a better job on his own. Just after I graduated from college, Taylor called and said he wanted me work alongside him, but the school didn't have the budget to add the position. So he went to the business office and cut a deal: if I was willing to work part-time in the business office and part-time in the dean's office with him, the school would hire me.

Taylor was in my corner from the beginning. He allowed me to recruit the RAs (resident assistants) that I would be comfortable working with, knowing that he could easily pick whom he wanted. He then allowed me to train them, something he had done hundreds of times and was much better at doing. But he wanted me to gain the experience, and that meant moving to the sidelines and giving me opportunity.

Taylor and his wife, Jimmye, are a dynamic ministry team. To this day, after I spend time with them, I feel like I could charge hell with a water pistol.

Much of what I try to practice in my discipling relationships comes from things I learned and experienced with Taylor, and the Lord has kept me learning throughout the years. Here are a few of my chief observations about the priorities and potential challenges of relating with disciples.

Serving

Serving your disciple is basic and absolute. In order to cultivate within the heart of a disciple the longing to follow Jesus, he must see genuine love and humility on display. Unlike worldly models of leadership, the discipler serves the disciple. Jesus himself exemplified this; he not only taught about a servant's heart, he demonstrated servanthood in daily living.

As I mentioned in an earlier chapter, it's interesting to me that when evangelicals wrestle with ministry-related issues or seek to start new churches and outreaches, we instinctively turn to the books of Acts and the Epistles for guidance, often overlooking the four Gospels. Yet it is in these books—Matthew, Mark, Luke, and John—that we find the account of Jesus training his twelve disciples to advance the kingdom of God. This is not to say that the other New Testament books do not contain essential truth for us today, but it is in the Gospels that we learn what it means to be a follower of Jesus and where he demonstrates for us how to develop the lives of those who will follow him. I propose that we broaden our study with a fresh look at the Gospels as an essential guide to kingdom ministry.

Take even a quick glance at the relationship that Jesus had with the twelve, and you'll know that disciple-making requires more than a weekly Bible study at Starbucks. Discipleship is, to borrow a phrase from Dietrich Bonhoeffer, *life together*. In practical terms this means that I should become acquainted enough with the life of my disciple to recognize opportunities to serve him. I must be available. (Incidentally, this is why I believe that we can only effectively disciple a limited number of people.) What good is it if I am aware of my disciple's needs, but am regularly unavailable to help because of my overcommitment?

Conflict

There's a story of Jesus and his disciples that makes me smile every time I read it. They were getting settled into the house after a trip when Jesus asked the disciples, "What were you arguing about on the road?" The disciples could only answer with silence because they were ashamed to admit what Jesus already knew—they had been arguing about which one of them was the greatest (Mark 9:33-34). Busted!

Yes, we'd like to think in any group of believers, such conflicts wouldn't occur. We know, as followers of Jesus, we possess a particular way of relating to one another and living out our lives together. That "way" is to consider others more important than ourselves and to serve them—to look out for their needs more than we do our own. Sure, that kind of love and humility is idealistic at times, but it should always be our goal.

I'm a realist, though, and I know that any group of two or more—even a tight-knit discipling community—will eventually face conflict. But I also believe this: conflict does not have to be a disruption; it can be an opportunity.

Returning to the story of the arguing disciples, watch how Jesus used their discord as a teaching point.

> Sitting down, Jesus called the Twelve and said, "If anyone wants to be first, he must be the very last, and the servant of all." (Mark 9:35)

I don't think Jesus was yelling when he said this. That the disciples were prideful and argumentative came as no surprise to him. He knew who and what they were when he chose them. So on those occasions, like this one, when the depravity of their nature overshadowed the grace that was at work in them, Jesus said, *Wait! There's a better way. A kingdom way.* And he then went on to instruct them, by explanation and demonstration, how to live.

Be watchful of conflict and be prepared to train your disciples through it. This is when they can learn some of the most significant life lessons—forgiveness, humility, genuine love, praying with intensity, not spreading gossip, being patient. Don't waste these moments.

Manipulators

One key role you'll need to be prepared for as a discipler is that of protector, or soul guardian. The relationship you have with your disciples is largely parental in nature, and this means that you will sometimes need to protect them from toxic people. In my experience, the most life-sapping people—from a spiritual and emotional perspective—are manipulators.

Manipulation is a form of control. Quite often controlling people are easy to spot because they tend to be brash and opinionated; their agenda is obvious. However, manipulators use a different playbook altogether. They are no less controlling but far more cunning. Manipulators are masters of subtlety, often masquerading as victims to hide an inner sense of moral superiority. A manipulator can disguise his actions so shrewdly that few recognize his true intent. And even if his motives are questioned, the manipulator can convincingly deflect the blame onto other people who have allegedly wronged him or onto circumstances that wounded him. Manipulators rarely see themselves as being in any way responsible for their issues.

The poison of a manipulator is that he will likely disrupt and even neutralize most of your disciple's other relationships with family and friends. By subtly driving a wedge between your disciple and the other people in his life—through monopolizing time, playing on sympathies, or threatening to "unfriend" him—the manipulator gets what he wants: control. A veteran manipulator can deceive so well that when your disciple's other relationships do become detached, he will probably believe that those people, not the manipulator, are the problem.

Please, step in before this happens. You see, precious few people can untangle themselves from the web of a manipulator without help. And in the discipler-disciple relationship, that help is you!

Because manipulation is the antithesis of love, one of the tools I use to help my disciples who are dealing with it is 1 Corinthians 13. Here the Bible gives a clear and understandable picture of love, which we can use as a measurement against the corrosive behavior of manipulators. I discuss with my disciple each of his closest and most influential relationships, both past and present, with an eye open for manipulators. Since manipulators have brought a certain amount of regret and even shame to the heart of my disciple, I often encounter reluctance, procrastination, and excuses when he begins to deal with these relationships and what they should look like going forward. In some cases it means breaking off a friendship or even an engagement, or it may require a confrontation and/or setting boundaries, all within the scope of genuine biblically defined love.

Often, manipulators are from your disciple's past and are no longer on the scene. Still, it is important to understand that manipulation casts a long shadow, and you may need to explore some past key relationships to understand how they may still affect his thinking and behavior. It could be that a parent, grandparent, girlfriend, teacher, or coach said or did things years ago that still drive the way your disciple sees himself and the world to this day. I once discipled a college student named John whose outlook was tarnished by a statement made to him by his second grade teacher: "You can't seem to do anything right." For years, her perception was John's reality.

But what about the manipulators themselves? Are they just to be cast aside and forgotten? Absolutely not. In fact, on more than one occasion the manipulators that I've had to deal with have themselves been part of our discipling community. I have a responsibility for them as well. But that means that I cannot let them continue to relate to others in this toxic way. They are hurting themselves as much as they are hurting others, perhaps more. Their inability to love well says to me that they are not receiving love well either, and this is a breakdown in their relationship with God and others that I am more than willing to help them work on. So I throw them a rope too. I offer to help them, but they must first be willing to "own" their manipulative ways.

How long?

In the next chapter we'll talk about some very practical issues about how to get started with your disciple, but before moving on I want to quickly address a question that I'm often asked about the discipler-disciple relationship: How long should I stay with a disciple, especially when there doesn't seem to be any progress?

These relationships are as unique as the personalities involved, times two. But it's important that you accept the fact that life-change and spiritual multiplication will take longer than you think it will. And you'll have to be patient. Jesus served the twelve for three years, and yet on the night before his crucifixion the disciples were still debating among themselves who was the greatest (Luke 22:24).

Making a genuine discipleship commitment to another person should not be thought of as a time-restricted arrangement. Sure, the day will come when the nature of the relationship changes and the two of you will not spend as much time together. But once your lives connect this deeply, you're in it for life. When is your disciple no longer your disciple? . . . When is your son no longer your son?

Nate's Story

My journey of disciple-making has taken interesting turns. I was first exposed to disciple-making by my youth pastor when I was a teen, probably without realizing what was really happening. Unfortunately, being a pastor's son and seeing the ugly side of church politics, I saw a lot of actions contrary to the law of love that has caused confusion and made me feel disillusioned. Though I'm still working through some of that, I finally met someone after I graduated who put words to what I was feeling. I prayed that God would show me what it meant to make disciples before I graduated because I realized I had no clue what it meant, yet I was telling people this was what I wanted to do. Then I met Lewie, and over a year's time gained a much clearer understanding.

I've learned that discipleship is the act of loving a brother or sister with the love of Jesus. I always knew love had a huge part in a believer's life, but it was more of an abstract concept for me that never played out in reality, though I held it as an ideal and hoped that it would. With Lewie and my friends in Chicago, I began to see that it could be a commonplace activity, and I soon realized that love is not just a huge part of a believer's life, it is *everything*. Love requires the death of my desires, the laying down of my life for my friends in the family of God. The idea that "love pursues" has changed the way I see people. People want to be pursued because then they feel that their life matters to someone.

7

The Timeline

Had it not been for a handful of pestering friends, I doubt that I would have ever written this book. For years they had been after me to "put what I do in writing" so others could learn how. I was reluctant because I wasn't sure that another book on discipleship was needed, but more so because I've never believed that genuine discipleship can be reduced to formula and process. However, God used their persistence (which is a nicer way of saying "pestering") and my own assurance through prayer that a helpful book could be written—if for no other purpose than to push me to analyze more carefully the *why* behind the *what*.

Over the past thirty-plus years, God has allowed me the privilege of being in hundreds of discipler-disciple relationships. And while I'm not given to linear thinking, at least when it comes to ministry (do A, then B, and you'll arrive at C), I have come to accept the fact that in order to train others in disciple-making a certain degree of process is necessary. So I'm turning a corner in this chapter. What I've written thus far has been more tactical than practical, more heart than head. And while I have no intention of changing those priorities, I will take on a more how-to approach beginning now.

So, when you find yourself sitting across the table in a local coffee shop, looking into the eyes of that young man who has asked you to disciple him, here are some suggestions for what to do next.

Getting to know your disciple

By the time I've agreed to disciple someone, I've already committed myself to the relationship in several key ways. For example, I've already begun to pray for him, have made myself available to him, and am beginning to look for practical ways to serve him. But now, as we move into new relational territory, I'm seeking to understand him.

This is what I mean by *knowing* your disciple, going beyond casual awareness of details that almost anyone could know (e.g., hometown, education and career training, marital status, etc.) and into the heart zone where hopes, fears, regrets, and dreams reside. As I set out in this relationship, I'm looking for the big answers to certain questions:

1. Who are you and how did you get here?
2. Where do you want to go in life and what's your plan to get there?
3. What's hindering you?
4. What can we do to help you? (Remember, he's coming into a community of disciples.)

I don't necessarily ask these questions verbatim. They mostly provide a framework for our interaction. (The more time we spend together, and the more I get to watch him interact with others, the clearer the answers to these questions become and the more I understand just who my disciple really is.)

Listening well

Next to love, nothing you can give your disciple is of greater consequence than listening to him. I suppose this could be said of all relationships. Paul Tillich writes, "The first duty of love is to listen." Yet how rare is it to have someone truly listen to us, even on occasions that should be marked by love?

Seminaries, colleges, and ministry-training courses teach us how to preach, teach, administrate, and lead, but not how to listen. Parachurch ministries spend thousands of dollars and work hundreds of hours trying to convince people to listen to what they have to say. But the real challenge of listening is that it requires a relationship, whereas preaching, teaching, and outreach can be done in nonpersonal ways. In the New Testament, both Jesus and Paul demonstrated how kingdom ministry should be done relationally. Jesus lived among his followers for thirty months and called them his friends (John 15:15). Paul loved the disciples at Thessalonica so much that he shared not only the gospel with them but his life as well (1 Thessalonians 2:8).

Listening is one of the first skills that should be developed when learning how to make disciples because listening to a person is foundational to understanding him. As your disciple begins to share his life story with you, it is vital that you listen intently, searching for ways that God has been at work throughout his life. Your aim, then, is to help your disciple join in the Lord's purpose for his life. As a discipler, you have no other agenda.

Building a timeline

You've probably seen a timeline used to diagram the sequence of key historical events. A timeline can be quite telling because it reveals the degree to which an event changed the course of history and the affected people or nation. For example, if you were using a timeline to analyze the growing popularity of the automobile in the U.S. over the past hundred years, you would conclude that the development of the assembly line in the manufacturing process was a history changer. As the assembly line was perfected, cars became more available and more affordable, and thus more popular.

Personal timelines can be equally insightful. I've discovered that drawing a timeline of my disciple's life—a personal history—is of great help in understanding him and knowing the direction that our discipling relationship needs to take. A timeline shows me the key events and circumstances that have shaped him (timelines reveal both positive and negative outcomes), and how God has been working in his life up to the present. Almost as soon as we begin meeting together regularly, my disciple and I start drawing his timeline.

I recommend this exercise to anyone who is starting out in a discipler-disciple relationship. Here are some things to keep in mind as you proceed.

- Developing a timeline takes time. Do not expect this to be complete after one or a few meetings. It will likely take weeks, or even months.
- You are looking for insight, not just information. Remember, this is being done for the purpose of *knowing* (understanding) who your disciple is.
- Begin the timeline wherever your disciple's memory is clearest. Don't feel that you have to start with his earliest years. You can always go back and fill in the gaps later.
- Take good notes but keep them safe and confidential.
- This exercise is a trust-builder, so be trustworthy.
- Expect some reluctance in talking about certain things. Be as patient with your disciple as you would want someone to be patient with you.
- Listen for what's not said. There may be topics or people that should be present but are conspicuously absent. For example, if your disciple says a lot about his mother but hardly mentions his father, this may indicate a strained relationship or even a deep wound.

Here is an example of a timeline. For the sake of space, I've included very little detail. The one you build with your disciple will likely show much more.

1990		Birth
1995		Death of Grandmother
1995-2002		Taft Elementary School
2000		Mean 4th grade teacher
2000		10th Birthday Surprise Party
2003		Lane Jr. High School
Oct. 2004		Cut from Basketball Team
2004		Bad Friends
Nov. 2004		Caught Stealing
Sept. 2005		Wilson High School
June 2006		Mission Trip to Haiti
Nov. 2006		Move with Mom to New City New High School - North Central High School
Summer 2007		New Youth Group & Pastor - Great Guy!
June 2008		Graduated from High School
Oct. 2009		D.W.I. - Jail Overnight
Jan. 2010		Dad Remarries
June 2011		Graduated Nursing School

After completing the timeline, I ask for one week to consider it and to pray through the life events of the disciple. Essentially what I'm looking for is the work of God throughout my disciple's life. His successes may indicate the ways that God has gifted him and could shed some light on his life's purpose. His sufferings could indicate places where healing is needed or ways that he can relate to and help others (2 Corinthians 1:4). His failures and fallings, especially if there is a pattern or similarity to them, is generally a warning of the ways that he will continue to battle temptation and the areas where he stands to learn much about God's grace.

As I said, a timeline can be very telling. It becomes a sort of personalized map of where our discipleship will go.

Unpacking your disciple's childhood

Don't be surprised that some of the most enlightening circumstances and events you and your disciple uncover during the timeline-building process will have occurred in his childhood. In fact, it is helpful to keep in mind just how greatly childhood affects a person's basic outlook on life. C. S. Lewis observed, "I fancy that most of those who think at all have done a great deal of their thinking in the first fourteen years."[1] I agree.

Understand that God has been at work fulfilling his purpose throughout the entire life of your disciple, and that God is no less present in childhood than he is in adulthood. However, recalling childhood memories, sharing them with another person, and understanding their significance can be challenging. A few of the lessons I've learned about helping my disciple unpack his childhood include:

- Be extra-sensitive. Childhood memories can still carry with them the sting of fear, shame, and inadequacy.
- While listening to a successful and confident adult, it is easy to pass over seemingly insignificant childhood events (like the strikeout story in chapter 1), when in reality these may have been defining moments in his life. If he gets more emotional than usual in telling it, or if you feel a heightened degree of emotion yourself in hearing it, chances are this is an event the two of you need to discuss further.
- Do not prejudge which events are significant or which ones are ordinary in the life of a disciple. For example, a parent's divorce may not carry the same weight to a child as being taunted or bullied at school, strange as that may seem.
- People will intentionally skip over painful childhood experiences until they know they can trust you. Over the months, as the trust between you and your disciple builds,

he will find the courage to share some of these more difficult experiences with you.

- When possible, ask your disciple to indicate when he is telling you something from his childhood that is important. Some stories are just memories while others are life-shapers. Often, the disciple already knows which is which.

Trust is a must!

Patience and trust are necessary when building your disciple's timeline, just as these qualities are at the core of the whole discipler-disciple relationship. Most children of God have not had anyone help them interpret the experiences of their life. Although they may have had family or friends who have listened, few have had anyone with the spiritual insight to help them see the Lord's purpose in their life circumstances. Often a person will be intimidated to have someone genuinely listen to them for the first time. It is not unusual to take months for trust to be built between the discipler and disciple.

By asking questions and then giving him plenty of time to answer, I teach my disciple to be "listened to." It is important for both the discipler and the disciple to be comfortable in silence. In the silence is where the disciple can formulate his answers as well as work up the courage to give the answer. Often the disciple will know the answer to the question but needs time to muster up the courage to say it out loud.

Beyond childhood, there are two other seasons of life that shape us more than most. We'll look at these, and their significance to discipleship, in the next chapter.

Jeremy's Story, Part 1

I was new to Moody Bible Institute in Chicago and didn't have any established friends. Ryan kept reaching out to me for reasons I couldn't at that time explain. In the beginning I turned down his overtures because I was afraid he would wear me out (maximum extrovert vs. a moderate introvert). But one day I said yes—ostensibly to make him stop asking.

I went to his place for dinner. There I met Toussaint, Khalid, Michael, and Lewie. We shared a meal together and they asked me to share my story with them. I remember being taken by the fact that they listened well, displayed interest in what I was saying, and asked questions. I felt welcomed and accepted. It seemed apparent that they belonged to each other and they weren't giving me signals that I didn't belong. I so enjoyed my time with them that I really didn't want to leave. But being a procrastinator by nature, I had a lot of homework to get done before the next day. I shared by dilemma with them: I don't want to leave, but I have to. But I'm afraid I will never experience "this" again. They laughed and assured me I would.

Lewie called a few days later and asked if I would like to get together. I don't remember what we did, but I remember he asked questions that made me think hard, and he delved deeper into my story than I had shared a few nights previous. Lewie also learned that I really enjoy exploring so he would often invite me along on an adventure to explore a section of town, a building, a church . . . it didn't matter, it was a shared adventure. We had fun, and in the midst of that, we shared life.

One of the things that really stuck out to me was that Lewie prayed for me every day. What an encouragement to know that in the midst of the difficulty, drudgery, or joy of the day, there was someone prevailing on heaven on my behalf.

As Lewie demonstrated consistency of character and a continuing interest in my life, I was willing to share more of myself with him. I remember the fateful day when I shared my biggest wound with him. We were sitting at Starbucks, and despite the fact that I knew he loved me and cared for me, it still took all I had to share it with him. But once it was out there, nothing changed between us. He didn't treat me according to what had happened to me.

Lewie also didn't confine our interaction to weekly one-on-ones or our group gatherings. He invited me into his life and let me share in what was going on. At first, letting me in made me know I belonged. Later, letting me in allowed me to serve and join in what he was doing.

As our friendship continued to grow, I became less introverted—perhaps realizing this wasn't necessarily how God made me, but how circumstances had. I haven't become a raging extrovert (like Ryan), but I have learned that fear shouldn't control my interactions and that love and concern for others coupled with obedience to God's commands makes me brave. Brave enough to risk getting hurt in reaching out to others.

8

Defining Moments

Ray and Kelly were part of our discipling community in Chicago. When God began to put it on their hearts to move to Portland, Oregon, our group helped them plan and fund an exploratory trip. We connected them with our contacts in the Northwest (family members, pastors, and friends) to help with housing and research in preparation for their move. We also put together a prayer card and informative letter encouraging others to join us in praying. Many people voluntarily gave money to help with moving expenses. We all wanted Ray and Kelly to know we fully supported them in their transition.

Transitions are passages that lead us from one place to another, from one assignment to the next. Transitions, even when they lead to something good, are often disruptive and, at least for a while, unsettling. Lives that had been running smoothly can begin to feel out of control when changing jobs, moving to a new city, getting married, counting down to retirement, or facing the empty nest. And though some transitions, like Ray and Kelly's, allow time for processing and planning, others are abrupt and uninvited.

On Friday, August 28, 2009, I was told that I had cancer. While sitting in the waiting room at the hospital, I had rehearsed in my mind how I should respond to the doctor if he came bringing bad news. (I had been a pastor, so mine should be a deeply spiritual response, right?) But as soon as the word "unfortunately" came out of the doctor's mouth, all self-composure fled and I went numb. The friend who had driven me to the appointment walked with me across the street to a park where we prayed and I cried.

After calling my family and friends that afternoon to let them know the diagnosis, I was emotionally exhausted. I told my friends I just wanted to be alone with the Lord, but later in the evening I received a phone call from a distraught young man whom I had been discipling. Lloyd's parents had just told him they were separating, and he asked if I could come pick him up from work. The last thing I wanted to do was drive in city traffic and pick up Lloyd. *Lord, of all nights!"* I thought. *"You know I love Lloyd but I have enough trouble of my own right now.*

After some tug-of-war with God, I did go and pick up Lloyd. As we rode down Lake Shore Drive together, I listened to his fears and anguish. Rather than resenting Lloyd's intrusion into my sorrow, I found myself listening to him with a new empathy because of my own heartbreak that day. Looking back I see that evening as a spiritually defining moment in Lloyd's life as well as in our friendship. And it was the first of many lessons that I would learn through a season of personal suffering. The Lord in his wisdom knew exactly when and how to mesh my pain with Lloyd's. (What are the odds that I would be diagnosed with cancer the same day that Lloyd's parents would separate?)

Worth the pain

Though we resist it, suffering is both the means of discipleship and the qualifier of disciplers. Remember what Paul wrote in 2 Corinthians 1:6? "If we are distressed, it is for your comfort and salvation; if we are comforted, it is for your comfort, which produces in you patient endurance of the same sufferings we suffer." The kingdom of God advances through our sufferings. This began with God himself and continues through us.

We see God's suffering throughout the Bible, beginning with Adam and Eve. Though God created them for the enjoyment of relationship, they rejected God and chose to live selfishly. Later God chose the nation of Israel to be his people, but they too rejected him and twisted his good intentions to appear as if he were malicious. Then at the death of Jesus we see the suffering heavenly Father as well as the suffering Son. At the cross, where suffering and love intersect, the way of real discipleship is revealed. God demonstrates his willingness to suffer in order to deliver those he loves from death to life.

The suffering of God overflows into the life of his followers. And only as we, as disciplers, have a heart like his—willing to sacrifice—are disciples made. Are we called to make disciples? Then a measure of suffering is sure to come. And this suffering will transform not only ourselves, but also those whom God has entrusted to our spiritual care.

> I tell you the truth, unless a kernel of wheat falls to the ground and dies, it remains only a single seed. But if it dies, it produces many seeds. (John 12:24)

> My command is this: Love each other as I have loved you. Greater love has no one than this, that he lay down his life for his friends. (John 15:12-13)

As painful as our own suffering is, watching those we love suffer—whether physically, emotionally, relationally, or whatever—hurts even more. A basic sense of compassion drives us to want to intervene and do something to lessen their pain. Even if they are partially to blame for their circumstances, love compels us to step in and rescue. But more often than not, we can't. We can, however, help them see the purposes of God in suffering.

The Suffering Chart

Allow me again to get quite practical, much like we did in the previous chapter. Similar to developing a timeline of your disciple's life, you may find this exercise equally enlightening.

The Suffering Chart (which I know sounds neither creative nor compassionate) is a way of helping your disciple discover the hurts he has encountered in life and the ways he has responded, for the purpose of seeing them as indications of how God is working to shape him. But this chart is not just for the disciple, it is for you the discipler as well.

The chart covers a three-year period. There is nothing magical about three years, other than the fact that it should be a sufficient amount of time for the disciple and discipler to begin recognizing sufferings and transitions for what they are—*spiritually defining moments.*

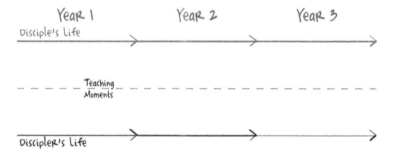

The top horizontal line represents the disciple's life, while the bottom horizontal line represents the discipler's life. The dashed line midway between the two indicates the place where the Holy Spirit causes the life of the discipler and the disciple to intersect, bringing them to teachable moments. Now let's add a little more detail.

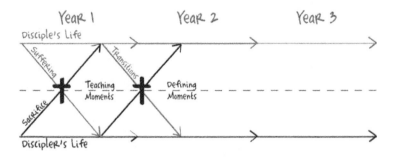

In the natural flow of life, your disciple will encounter suffering in some form (represented by the angled line so labeled). I accept and expect it because I believe that God is sovereign, and while this does not mean that I believe God is the *cause* of all suffering, I do believe he *controls* it. Therefore, suffering in the life of a Christ-follower is divinely purposeful and takes your disciple to a teachable moment. What he learns from his suffering, or *if* he learns from his suffering, is largely up to how you navigate him through it.

You will also notice a second angled line labeled "sacrifice." This one's for you, the discipler. Just as God uses the suffering of the disciple to bring him to a teachable moment, God will often call on you to sacrifice in some way to meet your disciple there to help him (see 2 Corinthians 1:5-6). Discipleship is rarely convenient and it sometimes hurts, even to the point of causing you to revisit some of your past pains—or encounter new ones—in order to empathize, love, and serve at a time when your disciple is vulnerable. You must join your disciple in his teachable moments.

I'll offer a few additional insights about this at the close of the chapter, but for now I'll say that your hope and prayer in these encounters of suffering and sacrifice is to escort your disciple toward God so that *teachable* moments become *defining* moments. Your disciple—and you, for that matter—should come out on the other side stronger in your faith. Discipleship will offer you many opportunities to relive your own experiences of sorrow and suffering for the sake of comforting your friend and reminding him that God is as near and as loving in the dark as he is in the light.

75

As you no doubt already know, in the matter of life-shaping challenges such as transitions and suffering, we are not one-and-done. There are always more teachable/defining moments ahead (as represented on the chart below).

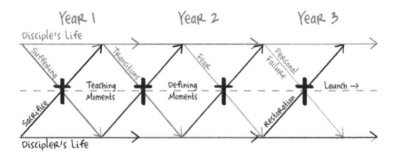

Hopefully, as I mentioned previously, three years of walking with your disciple through his sufferings will bring him to a level of maturity where he is not only able to recognize them for what they are and respond properly, but also where he is willing and able to offer the same help to others as you have offered him.

Keeping it all in perspective

Each disciple's life is an unfolding story of the gospel of Christ and the glory of God. This is a high calling, and one that we easily lose sight of when facing changes and challenges. It's not unusual for someone who has been growing in faith to become fearful and agitated when God starts to close one chapter and open another in his life. Because we can't see all that God is doing or what the outcome will be, our trust in him might take a hit. This then is the essence of your role as a discipler in these teachable moments, to remind your disciple of the character and nature of God. He may feel that God has changed; you need to assure him that he (God) has not. Show your disciple patience and understanding, and keep the following in mind:

- Transitions are rare, and therefore significant.
- Your disciple may be reluctant to make the transition, even when it's obvious that he should, because his current circumstances are familiar and comfortable. You may need to prod, reminding him that his life belongs to God, and God always knows best.
- On the contrary, your disciple may try to force a change because of discontentment in his present circumstances. Here you will need to remind him that each chapter of his life has purpose and that some chapters necessitate a deeper maturing, which requires waiting. Contentment, not change, opens the door to joy.
- Value transitions as times of faith-building. Much of what we really believe about God is formed in passing through these times, and we carry those beliefs into our next assignment.
- Understand the impact of transitions in your disciple's life. If it's a big deal to him, make it a big deal to you.
- Prepare yourself; the transition could affect you as well. Transitions can mean a separation between a discipler and disciple.
- Suffering opens your disciple's heart to the Lord and to you.
- The suffering of your disciple indicates the Lord at work in him, preparing him to make disciples.
- The lessons learned in suffering are for a lifetime. Just this week I was able to share with someone out of the suffering of my broken engagement, even though it occurred more than twenty years ago.

I'm often asked what curriculum I recommend for discipleship, and I've gotten more than a few curious stares when I've pulled out a pen and a piece of paper and started drawing the suffering chart. This is my curriculum. I know of no better way to connect with the heart of a disciple than to meet him in the crisis of faith—where he's wrestling to reconcile his pain with God's goodness—and explain to him what I've learned about God through my own hardships. As he hears me describe the blessings of my sufferings, he begins to see his own sufferings in a new light. More importantly, he understands more about the ways and purposes of God in his life.

Perhaps you should work through a suffering chart for yourself. I encourage you to do that before taking your disciple through one.

Jeremy's Story, Part 2

The powerful transformations that God was doing in my life through Lewie, our community, and of course the Holy Spirit became a driving force for the next step. If discipleship was so transformative in my life, then I should be reaching out to others with the same thing. I remember Lewie indirectly challenging me to think about such things. But I didn't do it because he told me to; rather it was like a fire in my bones that needed to be released, a sacred trust that needed to be invested in others, a Holy Spirit drive to fulfill the Great Commission. So I began to pray: *Lord, will you show me the guys you want me to disciple and make me brave to meet them and love them.*

Never before had an introvert gone to such lengths to strike up conversations with those around him. I met guys at the gym, developed relationships with coworkers, sat with strangers at meals, and even ran people down. I remember that Justin and I would pass each other in the parking lot quite often, and one particular time I felt a strong compulsion to talk to him, but I chickened out (which happened from time to time). So I prayed that if the Lord really wanted me to talk with him, Justin and I would cross paths again and I would strike up a conversation. Later that day, I noticed he was a good fifteen paces ahead of me in the lot, and I sped up behind him, said "Hi," which startled him (I was stealthy), and struck up a conversation. Over the years that followed, the Lord intertwined our lives and the lives of our spouses. Our friendship continues to this day.

In that first year, the Lord gave me about eight guys to disciple that I brought together into a community. We shared meals, the Lord's Supper, the Word of God, prayer, and our lives. We learned who we were, who God made us to be, and what was preventing us from getting there. We shared honestly where we had been and, for the first time in our lives for many of us, were loved in spite of our failures. Those relationships changed us deeply.

Over the years the guys have changed (because of graduation) and the numbers have fluctuated, but Julia and I still seek to use our home for hospitality as Lewie modeled for us. We seek to pour our lives into the lives of those around us and pray that we will see the Holy Spirit move in our lives and theirs. We continue to pray, "Lord, bring the right people and keep the wrong ones away."

Having kids has introduced a new dimension as we watch our children melt the hearts of the people around them and see the role they play in sharing the love of God. It hasn't always been sunshine and puppies. There have been times when our hearts have been taken through the wringer, either through the pain one of our disciples was going through or the pain they were inflicting upon us. Not every relationship has been a home run. There have been some bunts and foul balls along the way, but there have been enough guys forever changed that wherever we go, whatever we do, we will make disciples where the Lord plants us.

9

Heart-Mining:
200 Questions to Ask Your
Disciple

The purposes of a man's heart are deep waters, but a
man of understanding draws them out.

—Proverbs 20:5

Even after building a timeline and developing the suffering/
transition chart, there's still much ground to cover. This is when I
turn to the power of questions to stimulate ongoing and meaningful
conversations.

There's a great deal going on in the heart of your
disciple—memories, dreams, regrets, fears, hopes, questions, and
much more. Casual conversation and small talk will never get the
job done. Some people are more open than others, of course, and
you may find that getting your disciple talking is not difficult at
all. On the other hand there are many reasons why he might be
reluctant to open up to you. But the point is not just to get him
talking, but to get him talking about things that will help move
your discipleship forward.

This is what I call *heart-mining*—the process of discovering what is going on deep down in your disciple's emotions. Unless and until you get to that level, you're flying blind, not really sure what the issues are or where God is already at work.

Over the years I have developed and borrowed a list of questions that help me mine the hearts of those I disciple. I don't necessarily ask every person all of these questions, nor do I ask them in any certain order. But taking what I do know about my disciple, I select the questions that would seem to apply particularly to him.

I have listed the questions for you here, and following them are some general guidelines and observations about their use.

1. Have you noticed a pattern of God's movement in your life?
2. What might God be saying to you through the questions you have about him and about life?
3. What might God want you to hear through the events of your life?
4. Describe your prayer life and experience.
5. Who are the people who've had the greatest positive impact on you?
6. What characteristics do you most admire in people?
7. Are there any areas of your life that you want to hide from God?
8. What would you be willing to die for?
9. What have been the happiest moments of your life?
10. What is changing in you as you listen to God?
11. What about your life makes you feel trapped?
12. Who is the number one advisor in your life? Why?
13. What day of your life would you most like to relive? Why?
14. I am most like my mom in that I ___.
15. I am most like my dad in that I ___.
16. What would you choose if you had three wishes?
17. What is the nicest thing that anyone has ever said about you?
18. Where do you go or what do you do when life gets too heavy for you? Why?

19. I suspect that behind my back people say that I'm ___ because ___.

20. In what areas of your life would you like to have greater peace?

21. What are you passionate about?

22. What do you fear about the future?

23. Picture the first time you will stand before God. What do you want him to say about your life?

24. What would you really like to do and be?

25. What do you feel are your greatest strengths?

26. How do you want to be remembered?

27. What would you do if you had unlimited resources?

28. What is the one thing you could do that would have the greatest positive impact on yourself? On others?

29. Describe your uniqueness.

30. What energizes you and gets you excited?

31. What drains you of energy?

32. What are your abilities, skills, and talents?

33. Describe your present lifestyle.

34. Describe the lifestyle you'd like to have.

35. In what ways are you contributing to the common good?

36. When do you feel good about yourself and about life in general?

37. What are you doing when you feel God is working through you?

38. What makes you feel guilty?

39. What discourages you?

40. What necessary disciplines do you have (mental, emotional, spiritual, physical)?

41. What necessary disciplines do you lack (mental, emotional, spiritual, physical)?

42. How do you spend your discretionary time?

43. What recurring mistakes do you make that are becoming habits?

44. What is your genuine, sustained passion?

45. Describe your most pleasant memories. Your most painful.

46. What are your sources of motivation and inspiration?

47. What are your hobbies and most enjoyable forms of recreation?
48. What do you regret not having done in your past?
49. What spiritual disciplines have you found helpful?
50. Are you content with the person you are becoming?
51. Are you waiting to do something special in your life? Explain your answer.
52. Are you presently facing a difficulty? How is this difficulty and the way you are handling it shaping your life?
53. Do you have hopes of simplifying your life? How?
54. Is success in some areas of your life costing you too much in other areas? Explain.
55. Have you defined your non-negotiables (convictions you must live by no matter what)? What are they?
56. What image do you want to project about yourself? Is that image real? If not, in what ways is it not real?
57. Are you able to see the essence of situations and issues, or do you often get hung up on the peripherals?
58. Are you generous with your money, time, and possessions?
59. Are you able to respect yourself? Why, or why not?
60. Are you convinced that God loves you? Do you *really* believe it?
61. How do you react to change and transition?
62. Are you holding any grudges? Explain your answer.
63. Are you generally an optimist, a pessimist, or a realist?
64. What makes you feel secure?
65. In what areas of life do you often relapse?
66. Are you able to give and receive love easily? If not, what do you think hinders you?
67. Do you care what others think of you? Why, or why not?
68. What kind of power do you enjoy and utilize?
69. Have you generally accepted the person that you are?
70. Do you generally motivate people, or do you manipulate them?
71. Do you often play the role of God by attempting to punish yourself or others?
72. Are you able to discern and differentiate between spirituality and superstition?

73. What recurring temptations do you face?
74. List the five most important things that experience has taught you.
75. Are you able to help others develop and mature? In what ways do you help them?
76. Do other people ask for your advice? In what areas do they seek your advice?
77. What percent of your potential do you think you are using? Explain your answer.
78. Do you view the Bible as merely a guideline or as an authority?
79. Describe your personal relationship with Christ.
80. What words would friends and family members use to describe you?
81. How do you select friends?
82. Do you live more by a sense of responsibility or more by feeling?
83. Do you exercise financial discipline? Explain.
84. What habit(s) would you like to break?
85. What habit(s) would you like to make?
86. Is procrastination a problem for you? How so?
87. In what ways are you a role model for your children or for those under your care and influence?
88. What word(s) do you wish described you?
89. What specific progress have you made in the past year?
90. What actions are you taking based on faith?
91. What question(s) would you like to ask God?
92. In what ways would you like to change your attitude?
93. What changes would you make if you could live your life over thus far?
94. Name the one change that you would most like to make in your life.
95. What compliment do you most often receive?
96. What criticism do you most often receive?
97. What irritates you?
98. What situations make you feel insecure?
99. What experiences from your past still affect you the most?

100. Have you come to grips with death? Explain your answer.
101. How do you define love?
102. What is your greatest accomplishment in life thus far?
103. What do you do to promote harmony in your family and in your immediate circle of friends?
104. What do you look for in a role model?
105. How do you keep your mind active?
106. What intimidates you?
107. How do you generally respond to criticism?
108. Describe your three most enjoyable memories.
109. What effect does eternity have on your decision-making and planning?
110. List the three individuals who have influenced you the most.
111. Describe a time when you showed courage.
112. In what ways is life challenging for you right now?
113. When do you feel most alive?
114. How is God using you presently?
115. What is the greatest ongoing challenge in your life?
116. How well do you manage the ups and downs of life? What do you do to manage them?
117. What effect does faith have on your life?
118. Do your family members and friends know that you love them? How do they know?
119. What happens when you pray or meditate on Scripture?
120. What area of your life does God seem to be dealing with, or want to deal with, right now?
121. Are you missing anything in life that is important to you?
122. What does your name mean? Why were you given that name?
123. What was the best gift you received as a child?
124. What do you hope to contribute to the world?
125. What do you hope to be doing in ten years? Twenty?
126. What do you want to be remembered for?
127. What opportunities do you see unfolding for you?
128. What do others often ask you to do?
129. How do you define "accomplishment"?
130. What subjects interest you repeatedly?

131. Who do you enjoy spending time with?
132. Who and what commands your attention?
133. How do you escape boredom?
134. What concepts do you understand most clearly?
135. What keeps you from being what you want to be?
136. What things turn you off emotionally and spiritually?
137. How do you discern truth from error or falsehood?
138. What can you concentrate on at length?
139. What destructive weakness do you have? What are you doing to try fighting or overcoming it?
140. Do you have a basic philosophy of life? If so, describe it.
141. Describe some of the things you are currently doing to grow and mature.
142. What are your fantasies and how are they affecting or conflicting with reality?
143. Is your best impression made quickly or over a longer period of time?
144. How many long-term friendships have you maintained? What have you done to maintain them?
145. What triggers positive self-talk in you? Negative self-talk?
146. What interests would you like to develop?
147. Do you often waste time? What do you do when you are wasting time?
148. In what areas of life are you most disciplined? Why are these disciplines important to you?
149. How do you mesh the secular with the sacred in your life?
150. In what ways are you prejudiced?
151. What prejudices have you overcome?
152. Do you have an obsession that takes precedence over reason? Explain your answer.
153. What were you worried about a year ago?
154. Do you have a healthy sense of humor?
155. What is the most daring thing you've ever done?
156. What are you doing to encourage others?
157. Do others see you as you see yourself?
158. Do you seem to generate conflict often?

159. Do you have enemies? Who are they?
160. How do you generally handle confrontation—comfortably and in a timely manner, or by delaying it and letting the pressure build?
161. When do you want to be your own authority?
162. When do you feel free?
163. Do you feel that you have sufficient time for yourself? What do you do with that time?
164. Who are the authorities in your life and in what areas?
165. Do you know how to benefit from bad and hurtful experiences? Explain your answer.
166. Do you believe in heaven and hell? How does your belief affect your life and relationships?
167. What shortcuts are you tempted to take in life, and what are you hoping to avoid by these shortcuts?
168. How do you like for approval to be communicated to you?
169. In what ways are you and your spouse united as one? What are the major areas of recurring disagreement or conflict?
170. Are you more prone to remember the positive experiences of your life or the negative ones? Why do you think you do this?
171. Do you quickly accept responsibility for your mistakes, or do you often try to push the blame on someone else?
172. Do you demand theological closure to all issues, or are you able to live with some ambiguity?
173. Are you more of a critic or more of a coach?
174. If you were to die soon, what would be your legacy—what would you be remembered for? What do you want your legacy to be?
175. Describe your relationship with your parents or the people who raised you.
176. How do you decide who to spend time with?
177. How do you demonstrate gratitude?
178. What are your priorities, and how do you determine them?
179. What progress are you planning to make this year?
180. What do you do to be liked?

181. If needed, what could you do to reduce your standard of living?
182. What plans are you making for retirement years?
183. How do you control anger?
184. Describe a recent special experience that you enjoyed.
185. What problems has your ego caused for you and for others?
186. What do you feel makes life worthwhile?
187. What changes would you like to help make in your culture?
188. Describe the big life lessons you learned from your parents or those who raised you.
189. Have your grandparents been a significant part of your life? If so, what have you learned from them?
190. What can you do to improve your communication skills?
191. Do you ever attempt to justify lying and deception? Explain your answer.
192. Do you feel that you sometimes try to stifle emotions more than you should? Under what circumstances do you stifle them, and what is the result?
193. Do you enjoy what you are doing vocationally? If not, what changes would you like to make?
194. What have you done to try to improve your personality?
195. In what ways are you most influenced through peer pressure?
196. Do you have meaningful conversations? What makes conversations meaningful to you?
197. What traits have you inherited?
198. Have you ever had a change of heart or opinion on a major issue? Explain your answer.
199. What makes you thankful to be alive?
200. How do you know that God loves you?

Using questions

A few general thoughts about using questions in discipleship:

1. Be cautious about when you ask certain questions and how many questions you ask in one sitting.

2. You probably noticed that some questions overlap with others and are likely to get similar responses. Keep in mind that people communicate differently; what is clear to one person might be confusing to another. If one question doesn't get the information you need, you may want to ask the question differently. Think not only about how you ask, but how they will hear your question.

3. Conversation is essential to discipleship, so remember that asking questions of your disciple is for much greater purposes than curiosity or information-gathering. You are getting to know him, perhaps on a deeper level than he has allowed himself to be known before. And you are helping him see where God is working in his life.

Brent's Story

It's love. That is really the difference. I remember having dinner with Lewie and three others one evening after he spoke at our weekly collegiate worship gathering. He was asking questions of us all. When we were leaving, he suggested I call him to get together for lunch sometime soon. I didn't think he was serious. I had known pastors for years and never had one ask to have lunch with me. After all, "Let's do lunch" is a common moniker that really means "See you later."

A month or so later I found myself in the same situation, only this time Lewie said, "I never heard from you about lunch." He was serious about meeting with me. *Someone more mature in the faith, a pastor, wanted to spend time with me?* And so it began.

For our first lunch we met for pizza. We didn't talk about a sermon. We didn't read the Bible. Yet Lewie asked questions about things I had never spoken about to anyone. "Tell me about your parents." "Which of your parents are you more like?" He wanted to know my story. I didn't know how to tell it, but he knew how to get it from me. He considered me important enough to get to know. He figured the Father was at work in my life and wanted to find out how and why the Father had taken me on the journey I had been on.

Lewie was revealing my own heart to me by using my own words to help me see the Father's work in my life. He didn't mind asking unanswerable questions. "What do you think God's purpose was in allowing you go through your parents' divorce?" I had never considered God's involvement in the everyday accounts of my life, though I was the grandson of a preacher and had attended church three times a week for much of my life. I can only tell you of a few things I heard from the pulpit while growing up, but I can tell you about my first meeting with Lewie Clark. I can tell you that after our first meeting, I couldn't wait for our next lunch, or the next.

Growing up, I felt bad that I didn't enjoy church. I always felt something was missing. I had decided to just accept things as they were and stop asking questions. But Lewie told me he loved me, and I didn't really know what to think. On one hand it was great to have someone really care about you. On the other hand, it was so foreign to hear those words that I almost felt weird. Lewie had built trust with me so I took him at his word. I didn't know it at the time, but the Holy Spirit was showing me that brotherly love was what I was longing for.

Lewie's love and encouragement made me feel like I could walk through walls. After all, the Father is at work in my life. Why *shouldn't* I be able to accomplish what he has begun? I soon took a leave of absence from my job and went overseas for three months for a short mission trip. I have since gotten married, moved my new bride 1,500 miles across the country to help start a house church, stopped leading that house church, and am currently learning what it looks like to create a culture of faith in my family that spills over into the lives of the friends the Father has given us.

I have learned that my former understanding of following Jesus, talking (or listening) about Christianity, is easy but unfulfilling. Love, however, is hard. Love requires close relationships. Love is messy. I will be hurt. I will probably hurt others. I must help others see their story in the Father. I must help foster community among my brothers and sisters that far surpasses anything they could imagine. I must sacrifice, suffer, and pray. I must obey. I must love—love the Father, love my family, and love others. Without love, I am nothing.

10

Finding Your Disciple

Discipleship is in your heart. God put it there. You have the desire and hopefully you feel a bit more prepared for it than you did nine chapters ago. So, what now? If you didn't have someone specific in mind while reading this book, you're probably asking: *Who should I disciple?*

You're not alone in wondering. People who have a genuine heart for discipleship often stumble out of the gate because they don't know how to determine the person they should engage in a discipler-disciple relationship. And even though they often have a clear picture of what they hope the relationship will eventually become, they're at a loss for how to get underway.

At the risk of sounding simplistic, my answers to these questions are:

- *Who?* More than likely, the person God has for you to disciple is already in your life's orbit, or soon will be.
- *How?* To make a disciple, make a friend.

Location, location, location

As unspiritual as it may sound, one of the criteria I use before getting involved in a discipleship relationship is that the disciple and I must live in close proximity. Think it through a little more by considering: (1) how closely he and I need to be connected in the day-in-and-day-out of life and (2) how near and available I need to be when my disciple is suffering. This makes the idea of proximity not sound so unspiritual after all. Even though the world seems smaller than before, due to the advancement of Internet-based communication options, a video chat just isn't always enough.

Living in close proximity allows the discipler to serve the physical needs of his disciple and enables the discipler to witness how his disciple responds to the circumstances of life. In turn, the disciple has the opportunity to imitate his discipler by observing the way he lives out following Jesus (e.g., how he treats his wife and children, how he relates to others, and how he responds to suffering).

But there's also more at stake than the discipler and disciple's relationship; there's also the matter of the disciple's relationships with the other members of the discipling community. As I said in an earlier chapter, I no longer enter into discipleship with a person who is not also connected to a community of disciples. That being the case, proximity is not optional.

Jesus chose Capernaum to be his base of ministry, and he chose men to disciple who lived and worked in the same region. It's also interesting to note that Jesus did not remove these disciples from their family, friends, neighbors, and community. As a matter of fact, their spiritual formation took place in the midst of the environment in which they lived. It was at home where they learned to be disciples and to make disciples. Think of the significance of that statement as you read Matthew 9:10.

> While Jesus was having dinner at Matthew's house, many tax collectors and "sinners" came and ate with him and his disciples.

I wonder how Matthew's life changed after this unusual dinner party. Imagine the new opportunities that were opened up to him to spiritually connect with the people in his hometown, many of whom he'd probably never even noticed before.

Jesus was a real person, who lived in a real time and in a real place, and who came to demonstrate how to make disciples in the context of our family, our friends, and our hometown. He provided a model that everyone can emulate. There is significance to the place where God has put us.

Discipleship begins where you live. So when seeking a disciple, don't look too far from where you are.

Friends

If the place where God has put us is integral to discipleship, certainly the people who are part of our lives are there by God's doing as well. In fact, I don't believe it's possible to separate friendship from disciple-making.

Man did not invent friendship; God designed it. Friendship flows from his loving nature, and we see God extending himself to people throughout history. Abraham was called a friend of God (2 Chronicles 20:7-8; Isaiah 41:8; James 2:23-24). God would speak to Moses face-to-face "as a man speaks with his friend" (Exodus 33:11). God also demonstrated friendship through Christ. In addition to his friendship with Lazarus and various "sinners and outcasts," the Gospels give an extensive account of Christ's friendship with his disciples. They were his disciples and they were his friends.

So when I'm asked, "Where do I begin in making disciples of Jesus?" I always answer, "By being a friend." I don't announce to someone, "I'm discipling you!" Rather, I simply show an interest in his life, seek to find where God is already at work there, and join in the adventure.

If you want to know how effective you can be as a disciple-maker, ask yourself how good of a friend you are. The inability to make friends means an inability to make disciples, which in turn hinders the multiplication of the kingdom of God. This is no small matter.

Jonathan and David

Our view of friendship is often limited to people who look like us, come from similar social and economic backgrounds, share our interests, and are close to our age. Sadly, this perspective not only narrows our prospects for friends, but it also limits the extent of what a friendship could become and the influence it could have. I believe we need to widen our view to include people who are younger, older, and in other ways different from ourselves. The biblical account of the friendship between Jonathan and David is a helpful reminder.

Jonathan was the oldest son of Israel's King Saul. He was a distinguished warrior when he first met David, who was a teenage shepherd. (Although setting dates in ancient history is difficult, we can approximate that Jonathan was twenty years older than David.) Jonathan lived in palaces while David slept in open fields. Jonathan was the oldest son, David the youngest. Jonathan was married, and David was single. Jonathan was respected while David had lived with ridicule from his family.

I respect Jonathan; he lived counter to his surroundings and upbringing. His father was an angry, violent, irrational, and self-serving man. And while his siblings were shaped by their environment, Jonathan rose above it and to this day gives us an example of what a godly man and friend should be.

One thing we can learn about friendship, and thus about discipleship, from the life of Jonathan is that he was an initiator. He reached out to David in friendship by way of a covenant. A covenant was an agreement between two parties that set the conditions of the ongoing relationship. A covenant was not between equals; rather it followed the pattern common to the ancient treaties where the victorious king would set the terms of the covenant with the conquered people. The covenant implied relationship, promise, and expectation. At the beginning of their friendship, Jonathan, as the crown prince, initiated the covenant with David who, at that point, made no commitment to Jonathan.

In similar fashion, Jesus told his disciples that he had chosen them; they had not chosen him (John 15:16). It is life-changing to be pursued by love, whether in romance, friendship, or discipleship. As a discipler I do not wait for disciples to come to me. *I pursue them.*

Many desire a Jonathan-and-David friendship (or in keeping with the terms we've used in this book, a discipler-disciple relationship), but few are willing to pay the price. The starting point for such a friendship is a heart surrendered to the Lord. If I am not yielded to the will of God, not only will I have difficulty embracing God's purpose for my own life, but I also open myself up to jealousy and envy, even with those to whom I am closest. Jonathan exhibits for us a heart that is surrendered to the purpose of God, resulting in his extraordinary friendship with David, in spite of their circumstances.

As Jonathan and David's story unfolds, we see deeper into Jonathan's heart. He was in line to inherit the throne from his father, Saul, but due to Saul's stubbornness and disobedience, his family lost the right of succession. Jonathan's loss of the throne was due to no fault of his own, and yet he stayed submissive to the purpose of God even though it meant a lesser role for him. Not only was it a diminished role, but he submitted himself to the very man who was to take his place on the throne.

> And Saul's son Jonathan went to David at Horesh and helped him find strength in God. "Don't be afraid," he said. "My father Saul will not lay a hand on you. *You will be king over Israel, and I will be second to you.* Even my father Saul knows this." (1 Samuel 23:16-18, emphasis added)

Jonathan had the freedom to love and serve David rather than consider him a threat because he was surrendered to God's purpose in all things. Viewing others from a surrendered heart removes all threat and gives us the opportunity and privilege to lay down our lives for our friends, first out of our love for God but also out of love for our friends and disciples. Also, David could trust Jonathan because Jonathan's surrendered heart would never allow him to thwart God's plan. A surrendered heart finds joy in making others a success, no matter the cost.

As you set out to make disciples, I urge you to keep these lessons in mind. Your disciples are not your trophies or success stories. You are their servant. Your aim is to guide them ever closer to God and to his purposes for their lives. Eventually, your role will lessen and your contact with them will decrease.

Relate

The kingdom of God is about relationships. Man was designed by God to be loved and to love. The sad news is that in the Garden of Eden, Adam and Eve's relationships were shattered, both with God and with each other. Barriers of shame, self-consciousness, and fear grew up between individuals and between man and God.

The good news is that Jesus has reconciled man to God so that he can once again have a loving relationship with God and with others. Jesus came to earth to demonstrate how men can lovingly relate to God and to one another, both through his sacrifice on the cross and through the example of his thirty-month relationship with His own disciples. The discipling relationship restores individuals to God's design so that man can be in relationship with one another as the Lord intended.

Simply put, this is how a discipling friendship works:

1. God loved me first.

The reason I can love God and love others is because he first loved me (1 John 4:19). I am now able to love God and others out of the reservoir of infinite love poured into my life by God. Religion tries to manipulate men to love God, but the basis of the kingdom is that God loves us first and we are grateful responders to that love. "This is love: not that we loved God, but that he loved us and sent his Son as an atoning sacrifice for our sins" (1 John 4:10).

2. Relational restoration takes place in the bond of a discipling friendship.

A discipling-friendship relationship is a vital component in the kingdom because it is the means by which men learn how to love and to be loved. Jesus has given us the example of how to love by the laying down of his life for us. I am to love others in the same way by laying down my life for them. It is in a discipling friendship that I experience being loved and then also having the opportunity to love another.

So . . . Where do you find your disciple? Perhaps a better question is, Do you believe that God knows what he's doing? If you do, I suggest you take a good look at the place where he has put you and consider the people he has brought into your life. God has already been at work. Join him.

If you know how to be a friend, you already know most of what you need to be a disciple-maker.

Danny's Story

I successfully avoided Lewie Clark for a year and a half. The word on campus was that he could read minds, and I wanted none of that. I was in a place I didn't want to be—my dad had told me that if I'd go to Christian college for one year I could do whatever I wanted afterward. So there I was at Calvary Bible College just doing my time.

Lewie was the dean of men. Of course he couldn't really read minds, but he had a reputation for asking a lot of questions and drawing stuff out of a guy's heart. And I just wasn't all that interested in being known. I planned to do my year, keep my rebellion under wraps, and get on with my life my way.

I ended up taking a class in the same building where Lewie taught, so we would often run into each other and chat. I settled in to the casual nature of our friendship, and was no longer feeling quite so threatened until the day he extended the dreaded invitation: "Why don't you come by later and let's talk some more?"

I rehearsed all afternoon. Now I have to admit that I had been living in absolute sin the whole time. If Lewie—or any other administrator—knew what I'd really been doing, I'd have been kicked out. So I had to prep my answers—my lies—for Lewie in order to throw him off. Yet even at the same time that I was living in rebellion, God was drawing me. I had actually returned to Calvary for a second year, not because Dad made me but because I had begun to see something in the lives of people there that I wanted. In my heart I was going in two opposite directions.

So, Lewie and I sat down to talk and he asked how I was doing, what was going on in my life. And I launched in to my well-rehearsed answer. He let me go on for four or five minutes and then he looked at me and said, "When are you going to stop playing this game?"

Now a whole lot happened in that moment, and much of it is hard to explain. I do know that I was confident of two things: (1) God was speaking to my heart, and (2) God had put someone in front of me who would help me. The game-playing was over, and

I was glad. For the next three hours I poured out nineteen years worth of hurts, fears, and guilt.

I found out later that Lewie had been praying for me for most of the year and a half that led up to that conversation. He knew that if he approached me too soon I would not be ready to be honest, so he prayed and trusted God to work in my heart before approaching me. And when he did approach me he did more than simply confront me about the wayward life I was leading, he encouraged me with what he believed *would* be true—that God had kingdom related purposes for my life. Lewie also assured me that he would be there to help me.

That assurance became both the basis of our discipleship friendship and the foundation for my own disciple-making. Speaking truth *as if it were even though it is not yet* (in the spirit of Hebrews 11) is a great motivator to pursue and fulfill God's purpose.

Lewie discipled me intensely for eighteen months, through my remaining time at college. From the beginning I knew this wasn't really about me, it was about Christ and his plan for his kingdom to invade the world. I was being discipled to become a disciple-maker. God's plan was bigger than my dreams, and much bigger than my past attempts to derail that plan, at least as far as my life was concerned. Discipleship was not about getting my life together, it was about loving Jesus, loving people, and changing the world.

About eight months in, Lewie challenged me to begin praying that God would show me who I should disciple. By then I was looking at everyone through the lens of: *Is this a divine appointment? Is this someone I'm supposed to invest in?* Lewie had so instilled in me the realities of the sovereignty of God—that nothing happens by chance—that I was on the lookout for those God was bringing into my life for a longer-term discipleship investment.

After I graduated from Calvary I was hired on staff to work in public relations as a recruiter. (Ironic, isn't it? A few years prior I couldn't wait to get away; now I was staying past graduation!) And God brought to me a new student named Gary.

The following year God brought Lewie and me together again, this time on the staff of Life Action Ministries. Though this was a different ministry setting—we were part of a revival team that traveled throughout the U.S.—disciple-making was still very much our approach to the relationships we developed with our team members. During this time I really began to see the truth of something Lewie had been teaching me about disciple-making all along—that while I might have opportunity to teach and influence several people at a time, I could really only concentrate on a few. Just as Jesus had many followers, but seemed to have focused on Peter, James, and John, I learned that I had to be okay with that approach in my life. Even today, as a teaching pastor, I don't see myself as making disciples from the platform on Sunday mornings. That is a part of the process, but not where the primary work takes place.

A few years later God moved my family overseas to Slovakia, where I immediately went on the prayerful lookout for the man or men I was to disciple. This thinking drove my ministry, and drove my life. Still does.

Very soon God brought me into contact with Tomas, who at the time was just nineteen years old and in a difficult family environment. His life had been directed mostly by belittlement, manipulation, and humiliation, so we began with his having a very low level of trust in anyone older than he. I mention this because it was actually a very simple act that started bringing his walls down—I let him have a key to my office so he could use my computer to work on his term paper. This became a watershed moment. By handing him a key, Tomas felt that I had given him my trust which he received as a surprising demonstration of love.

In the context of the ministry I was doing at the time, it was natural to include Tomas in many of my activities. I often spoke at conferences, and would take him along with me. We had many great conversations driving the roads of Eastern Europe. And I took advantage of my need for help with the language, sometimes using him as a translator. I simply included him in what God had me doing.

Eventually Tomas began praying that God would bring a disciple-to-be across his path. I remember the day he came to me and said, "I know who it is! It's Andre." Andre was a sixteen-year-old boy who was at a very broken place in his life. Everything that I had done with Tomas, he began to do with Andre, and God began to transform Andre's life. This of course added a dynamic to my relationship with Tomas because we were not only talking about what was going on in Tomas's life, but also about what was going on in Andre's life.

And then Andre began asking God to point him to a disciple, and God brought Miso, who had just graduated from high school. Miso was spiritually lost, but he began hanging out in the café we had opened. After nearly two years—all the while Andre loving him and being his friend—Miso came to faith in Christ. He later joined our ministry team.

I could tell of many others, but I mention this particular "lineage" of four generations of disciples to make a point: Though Tomas is the only one of the men I've mentioned who's actually met Lewie, every one of them will say that Lewie has had a role in their life because of the influence he's had in mine. That's how it is with discipleship. Life is given and received and given and received and on and on and on.

Epilogue

For who makes you different from anyone else? What
do you have that you did not receive? And if you did
receive it, why do you boast as though you did not?
—1 Corinthians 4:7

I gave Danny what Taylor Gardner gave to me. And Taylor gave
to me what he had received from others. Discipleship is all about
passing along that which we've received. It's not mystical, it's
life. Christ's DNA being passed through humans. Life in Christ is
dynamic, a continuous production and reproduction of which we
are all a part. So please, stop asking *should* I be a disciple-maker or
can I be a disciple-maker and start asking *who* should I disciple?

Notes

Chapter 2

1. Robert Bellah, et al., *Habits of the Heart: Individualism and Commitment in American Life* (Berkeley: University of California Press, 1983), 84.

Chapter 3

1. Joseph H. Hellerman, *When the Church Was a Family* (Nashville: B&H Academic, 2009), 62.
2. Anne Morrow Lindbergh, *Hour of Gold, Hour of Lead: Diaries and Letters of Anne Morrow Lindbergh, 1929-1932* (Wilmington: Mariner Books, 1993), Introduction.
3. From the movie *Forrest Gump*

Chapter 4

1. C. S. Lewis, *God in the Dock: Essays on Theology and Ethics* (Eerdmans, 1994), 280.
2. Marla Paul, "The Friendship Crisis: Finding, Making, and Keeping Friends When You're Not a Kid Anymore" (Emmaus: Rodale Publishing, 2004)

Chapter 5

1. Delmar Paez, "The Missionary Dimension of Hospitality in The Third Gospel" (Maryhill School of Theology), 2.
2. Craig L. Blomberg, *Contagious Holiness: Jesus' Meals with Sinners* (Downers Grove: InterVarsity Press, 2005), 167.

Chapter 7

1. C. S. Lewis, *Surprised by Joy* (New York: Inspirational Press, 1987), 36.

Made in the USA
Coppell, TX
20 February 2022

73858904R00070